D0478537

CALGARY PUBLIC LIBRARY

SEP 2019

Bet You Didn't Know!
2

Only 20 lucky people a day are allowed to visit **the Wave** in Vermilion Cliffs National Monument in Arizona, U.S.A.

NATIONAL GEOGRAPHIC KIDS
Bet You Didn't Know!
2
Outrageous, Awesome, Out-of-This-World Facts
NATIONAL GEOGRAPHIC
WASHINGTON, D.C.

Contents

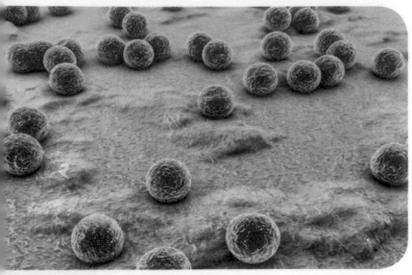

6 Eye-Popping Facts About Eyes

8 Fabulous Facts About Fashion

10 Wild Facts About Waves

12 Toothy Facts to Bite Into

14 What's the Difference?

16 Freaky Facts About Fungi

18 Shocking Facts About Lightning

20 Terrific Facts About Trees

24 Fishy Facts to Make You Move Your Fins

26 Contagious Facts About Viruses

28 One Gnarly Fact About the Blue Dragon Sea Slug

30 Facts About Birds to Tweet About

32 Sparkling Facts About Stuff That Shimmers and Shines

36 Surprising Facts About Seeds

38 Nifty Facts About Numbers

40 Strange Places: Polka Dot Lake

42 Amazing Facts About Arms and Armor

44 Soak Up These Facts About the Seashore

46 Shattering Facts About Glass

48 Rocket-Fueled Facts About Space

50 Facts That Totally Rock

52 Ultrahot Facts About Fire

54 Extreme Weirdness

56 Smooth Facts About Silk

58 Sugar-Coated Facts About Candy

62 Cosmic Facts About Constellations

64 Pizza Facts by the Slice

66 Cool Facts About Copycats

68 What's the Difference?

70 Radiant Facts About Rainbows

72 Dazzling Facts About Deserts

74 Facts About Lava to Warm Up To

76 Scaly Facts About Reptiles

78 Finger-Licking Facts About Peanut Butter and Jelly

80 Fluttering Facts About Butterflies

82 Dreamy Facts to Sleep On

84 Frigid Facts About the Arctic

86 One Majestic Fact About Castles

88 Picture These Facts About Photography

90 Squishy Facts About Slime

92 Outrageous Facts About Everything Under Our Feet

94 Strange Places: Stone Forest

96 Facts About Fur, Feathers, Skin, and Scales

100 Wild Facts About Places That Thrill

102 Alarming Facts About Deadly Animals

104 Music Facts to Get Stuck in Your Head

106 Extreme Weirdness

108 Facts About Survival to Keep You Going

110 Stinky Facts to Sniff Out

112 Weird Facts About Wild Animals

114 Birthday Facts That Take the Cake

118 Fast Facts About Wild Rides

120 Funky Facts About Fruits and Veggies

122 Spooky Facts About Haunted Places

124 Facts About Fun Festivals to Celebrate

126 Puzzling Facts About Unsolved Mysteries

128 What's the Difference?

130 Tricky Facts About Magicians

132 Extreme Facts About Adventures

134 Shhh! ... Secret Facts About Spies

136 Glowing Facts About Jellyfish

138 Funny Facts to Keep You Giggling

140 Itty-Bitty Facts About Tiny Animals

142 A Gallery of Amusing Facts About Museums

144 Strange Places: Striped Slopes

146 Bright Facts About Bioluminescence

148 Adorable Facts About Baby Animals

150 Fun Facts to Bear in Mind

152 Facts About Super Splurges

154 Action-Packed Facts About Sports

156 Relieving Facts About Ridiculous Restrooms

158 Extreme Weirdness

160 Heroic Facts About Daring Dudes

162 Heroic Facts About Gutsy Gals

164 What's the Difference?

166 Facts About National Parks to Explore

168 Fierce Facts About Vikings

170 Energetic Facts About Electricity

172 One Delightful Fact About the Dumbo Octopus

174 Futuristic Facts About Technology

176 Playful Facts to Monkey Around With

178 Amazing Facts About Roadside Attractions

180 One Towering Fact About Giraffes

182 Behind the Facts

182 Illustration Credits

184 Index

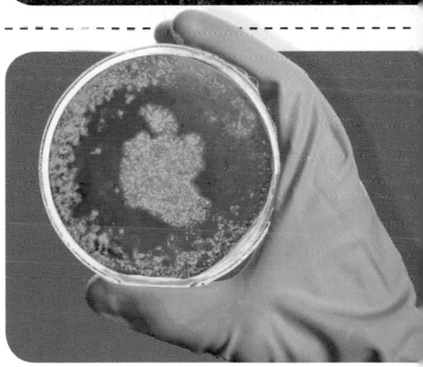

1

Predators such as snakes and cats tend to have **vertical pupils.**

2

Prey animals like goats and sheep tend to have **horizontal pupils.**

3

Doctors are testing an **implant** that will **help blind people see** in black and white.

4

Our eyes actually see the world **upside down,** but our brains **flip the image** so that it looks right side up.

5

Scallops, a type of shellfish, **have dozens** of **tiny blue eyes.**

6

Babies can **open their eyes** and recognize **face-like shapes** while they're still **in the womb.**

7

A **giant squid's** eyeball is as large as a **dinner plate.**

Eye-Popping Facts About Eyes

8

Some people are born with **special retinas** in their eyes that allow them to see **millions** of **extra colors.**

9

Looking at the **large eyes** of some baby animals can produce **chemicals** in your brain that **boost happiness.**

10

When **we stare** at something, our eyes actually move **back and forth** a tiny bit to keep the object **in focus.**

Fabulous Facts About Fashion

1

In Ancient Rome, only emperors and high-ranking officials could wear purple.

2

Necklaces and rings made from human hair were once popular fashion items in the United States and Europe.

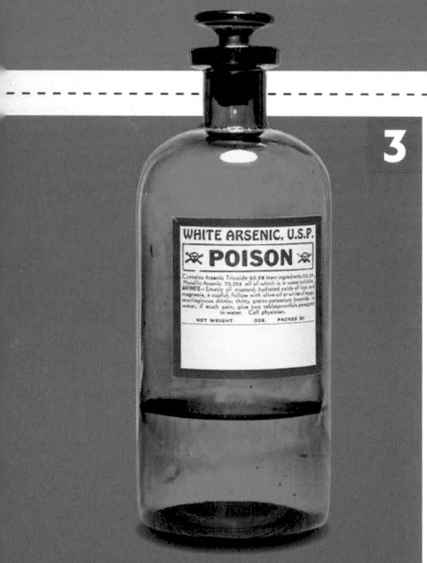

3

The poison arsenic was once used to dye fabrics green.

4

Models wear clothes made from chocolate at the Salon du Chocolat fashion show in Paris, France.

5

Worldwide, people spend an estimated $1.2 trillion each year on fashion products.

6

During Marie Antoinette's reign, women at the royal court were asked not to wear the same outfit twice.

7

Since astronauts can't do laundry in space, NASA scientists are testing the use of special exercise clothes that won't get smelly with wear.

8

A study showed that students who wear a Superman T-shirt during their exams may get better scores.

9

People once wore live lizards as brooches and hair accessories.

10

The world's longest wedding dress stretched for more than five miles. (8 km)

Wild Facts About Waves

1

The sound of **waves crashing** comes mostly from **air bubbles** in the water.

2

A **surfer** set a **world record** by riding a wave near Portugal that was as tall as a **seven-story building.**

3

Just like **the "wave"** that people make around a sports stadium, giant **honeybees** use a wave, called shimmering to **scare away hornets.**

4

Depending on the temperature and conditions, **sound waves** travel about **five times faster in water** than they do **in air.**

5

Doldrums are areas of ocean where there is sometimes **no wind or waves.**

6

When you are **thinking creatively,** your brain uses electrical signals called **theta waves.**

7

The **biggest tsunami** ever recorded was **1,720 feet** (524 m) **high,** which is taller than the **Empire State Building!**

8

There's a **deep layer** of cold water called the SOFAR channel that can **carry sound waves** for **thousands of miles—** even across entire oceans!

9

Satellites use **radio waves—** the same waves used to listen to a **car radio—** to communicate with scientists **back on Earth.**

10

Scientists can figure out what types of metals are deep **inside our planet** by studying earthquake **shock waves.**

Toothy Facts to Bite Into

1

Llamas have multiple sets of **sharp fangs** known as **"fighting teeth."**

2

Small sea snails called limpets have **teeth stronger than titanium.**

3

An extinct shark called *Helicoprion* had **teeth that rotated like a chain saw.**

4

Most **Americans** are familiar with the **Tooth Fairy,** but it's common for children in other parts of the world to **leave their baby teeth** out for a **mouse.**

5

Before **toothbrushes,** people used **"chew sticks"** to clean their teeth.

6

The **first toothbrush,** invented in China in 1498, used **boar bristles** to clean teeth. Toothbrushes with nylon bristles **weren't invented until 1938.**

7

Humans **can bite** with a force of up to **200 pounds** (91 kg).

8

Crocodiles bite down with **more force** than **any other living creature:** 3,700 pounds (1,680 kg), which is a little more than the weight of a **medium-size car.**

9

Tooth enamel is the **hardest substance** in the human body.

10

Cows, goats, and sheep **have no top front teeth.**

What's the Difference?

Check out these similar pairings and see how you can determine this from that!

FRECKLES VS. MOLES

Skin freckles and moles are a normal part of human skin, but some cultures have treated the spots just like hairstyles or anything else we wear. In the late 18th century, French aristocrats added fake beauty marks to their faces. The truth is that freckles and moles have nothing to do with fashion. Freckles develop when fair-skinned people spend a lot of time in the sun. The sun produces ultraviolet light, and when some people are exposed to it at a young age, skin cells on their bodies called melanocytes produce a pigment called melanin in small, uneven blotches that we call freckles. Meanwhile, moles are an overgrowth of melanocytes that form a little bump or flat circle, which some people are born with. The shape of our freckles and moles can't be changed at will. But whether you've got spots or not, your skin can be damaged by the sun, so make sure to put on sunscreen before you hit the beach!

SNAIL VS. SLUG

Hungry birds might be happy to see either of these slimy specimens in a garden, but the average gardener probably won't be pleased! Snails and slugs both have squishy bodies and leave a trail of slime wherever they go. They're both gastropods, a name that translates to "stomach foot." But these two creatures are not quite the same. Snails eat rocks and shells to ooze enough calcium carbonate to form an elaborate spiral shell that they can use for shelter and protection. While snails can retreat into their shells to stay moist, slugs have to head underground or beneath plants and trees to keep from drying out. Shell or no shell, these critters both devour just about everything in their path, but it takes them some time to chow down on budding plants and veggies. Far from speedy, slugs and snails travel at about .029 miles an hour (.0467 km/h). Now that's what you call a snail's pace!

SEA SNAKE VS. EEL

While both sea snakes and eels stalk the sea for snacks, sea snakes and eels are very different animals. Eels are found in both salt water and freshwater and are actually a species of fish, with fins and gills. Sea snakes, on the other hand, are water-dwelling reptiles that breathe air. Their bodies are shaped just like land snakes', and some species can spend several days at a time on land. Despite their differences, one thing's for sure: Both of these creatures can be dangerous. Sea snakes have some of the most toxic venom around. Eels, on the other hand, defend themselves with vicious teeth, and if it's an electric species, they can even give you a strong zap. If you find one of these wiggly beasts in the water or an aquarium, leave it be and watch it (from a safe distance) slither through its underwater world.

MARSHMALLOW VS. MERINGUE

How can you tell these two sugary-sweet substances apart? Early marshmallows were made with the marsh-dwelling mallow plant. The first modern version of the sweet showed up in 19th-century France, where sugar and egg whites were added to the plant's roots to create cough syrup or gummy vitamins. In the 1800s, production spread to the United States, where the plant extract was swapped out for a spongy protein called gelatin. The marshmallow changed once more in the 1950s, when a manufacturer pumped it up with air to make the squishy texture we love today. Meringue, however, is egg whites whipped with sugar into a fluffy topping or baked into a crunchy shell. Bon appétit!

TOMATO VS. TOMATILLO

Their names sound alike. You can make salsa out of both. And a tomatillo looks just like a tiny green tomato. So, are they the same? Turns out, the answer is no. Unlike tomatoes, tomatillos taste more tart and grow inside a papery husk that must be peeled away before they can be eaten. Tomatoes and tomatillos may be distant cousins of one another, but tomatillos are actually more closely related to gooseberries and ground cherries. The two plants are part of the deadly nightshade family, along with potatoes, peppers, and eggplants. Like all nightshades, the leaves and stems of the plants are poisonous. So, if you're trying to decide between tomatoes or tomatillos for your salsa recipe, whichever way you go, just stick with the fruit!

COMET VS. METEOR VS. METEORITE

You're stargazing and you see a bright streak in the night sky. It could be a meteor, also known as a shooting star, or it could be a comet. So, how do you know what to call it? Scientists often call comets "dirty snowballs" because they're made up of ice with bits of dirt, mud, and rocks held together in a tight ball. Comets also contain a blend of gases, including carbon dioxide, ammonia, and methane. When they streak across the solar system, the ice in the comet heats up and releases the gas and dust to form a long tail, which stargazers can sometimes see for several nights without a telescope. While comets put on a long show, meteors only make a quick stop and burn bright. Meteors come from meteoroids, which are small chunks from comets or other rocky objects in space. When meteoroids fly into Earth's atmosphere, they burn up as meteors, which is why you'd only spot them for a few seconds. To make things more confusing, if a piece of the meteor makes it through the atmosphere and lands on the surface, that's called a meteorite. So, if you're looking for a quick way to tell them apart, remember that comets are ice-cool and meteors rock.

Comet

Freaky Facts About Fungi

1

Truffle-sniffing pigs can find the expensive mushrooms even when they're growing three feet (1 m) underground.

2

The largest living thing in the world is a network of honey mushrooms that's about three times as big as New York City's Central Park.

3

Earth was once covered in giant, tree-size mushrooms.

4

Some mushrooms use an enzyme called luciferase to glow in the dark the same way fireflies do.

5

Fungi are more closely related to animals than they are to plants.

6

Scientists are using some mushrooms to develop new medicines.

7

Mushrooms contain a material called chitin, which is also found in insect, crab, and lobster shells.

8

Mushrooms can be used to make bricks and other building materials.

9

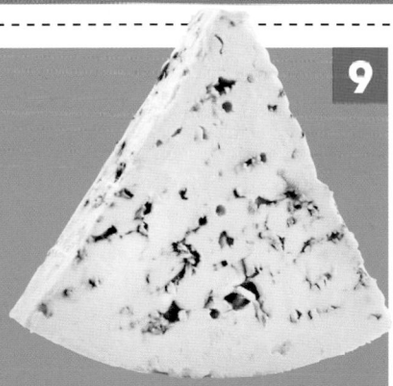

The veins found in blue cheese are caused by a type of mold.

10

A type of rainforest fungus infects the brains of ants, turning them into zombies and controlling the ants' every move!

Shocking Facts About Lightning

1

There's a lake in Venezuela where lightning strikes thousands of times a year.

2

Thunder is actually the sound of hot air vibrating around a lightning bolt.

3

A bolt of lightning is about five times hotter than the surface of the sun.

4

Scientists think they may have discovered "dark lightning," an invisible thundercloud energy burst that's less common and way more powerful than normal lightning.

5

Dozens of lightning strikes hit the Empire State Building each year.

6

One hundred lightning bolts strike our planet each second.

7

Lightning bolts are only about as wide as a person's thumb.

8

Most lightning jumps between clouds, rather than striking the ground.

9

"Ball lightning" consists of mysterious glowing spheres that seem to float or bounce along the ground for several seconds.

10

When lightning strikes the ground, it melts minerals into a bolt-shaped fossil called a fulgurite.

Terrific Facts About Trees

1

Birch trees "sleep" at night—their branches relax and droop when it's dark and perk back up in the morning.

2

Yellow-bellied sapsuckers are small woodpeckers that drill holes in tree bark and slurp up the sap that oozes out.

3

The fruit from Osage orange trees are sometimes called "monkey brains."

4

Arborists (people who take care of trees) compete for the **fastest climb** up a **60-foot** (18-m) tree at the International Tree Climbing Championships.

5

There are hundreds of **"moon trees"** in the United States—grown from seeds that **astronauts** once **sent into space.**

6

There's a **church inside** the **trunk of a tree** in France that's said to be **1,000 years old.**

7

People in the United States buy nearly **30 million Christmas trees** each year.

8

Dragon's blood trees bleed red sap when **they're cut.**

9

Thirsty trees make high-pitched **"slurping" sounds** that humans can't hear.

Turn the page for more tremendous tree facts!

10

There's a grove of giant, concrete-and-steel **Supertrees** in Singapore that capture **solar energy** and **rainwater,** just like **real trees!**

11

The **tallest tree** in the world, a **redwood** nicknamed "Hyperion," is taller than the **Statue of Liberty.**

12

Orangutans spend **most of their time** in trees.

13

The **poisonous** manchineel tree is called ***árbol de la muerte*** in Spanish, meaning **"tree of death."**

14

Trees "remember" events, even though they don't have brains.

15

The first species of tree appeared between 345 and 360 million years ago.

16

One of the world's oldest living things is a grove of aspen trees found in Utah, U.S.A. They're estimated to be at least 80,000 years old.

17

Trees give off chemical signals to warn each other about insect attacks.

18

In forests, neighboring trees "talk" to each other using an underground fungus called the "wood wide web."

19

One large tree can provide enough oxygen for four people every day.

20

Scientists who study tree rings are called dendrochronologists.

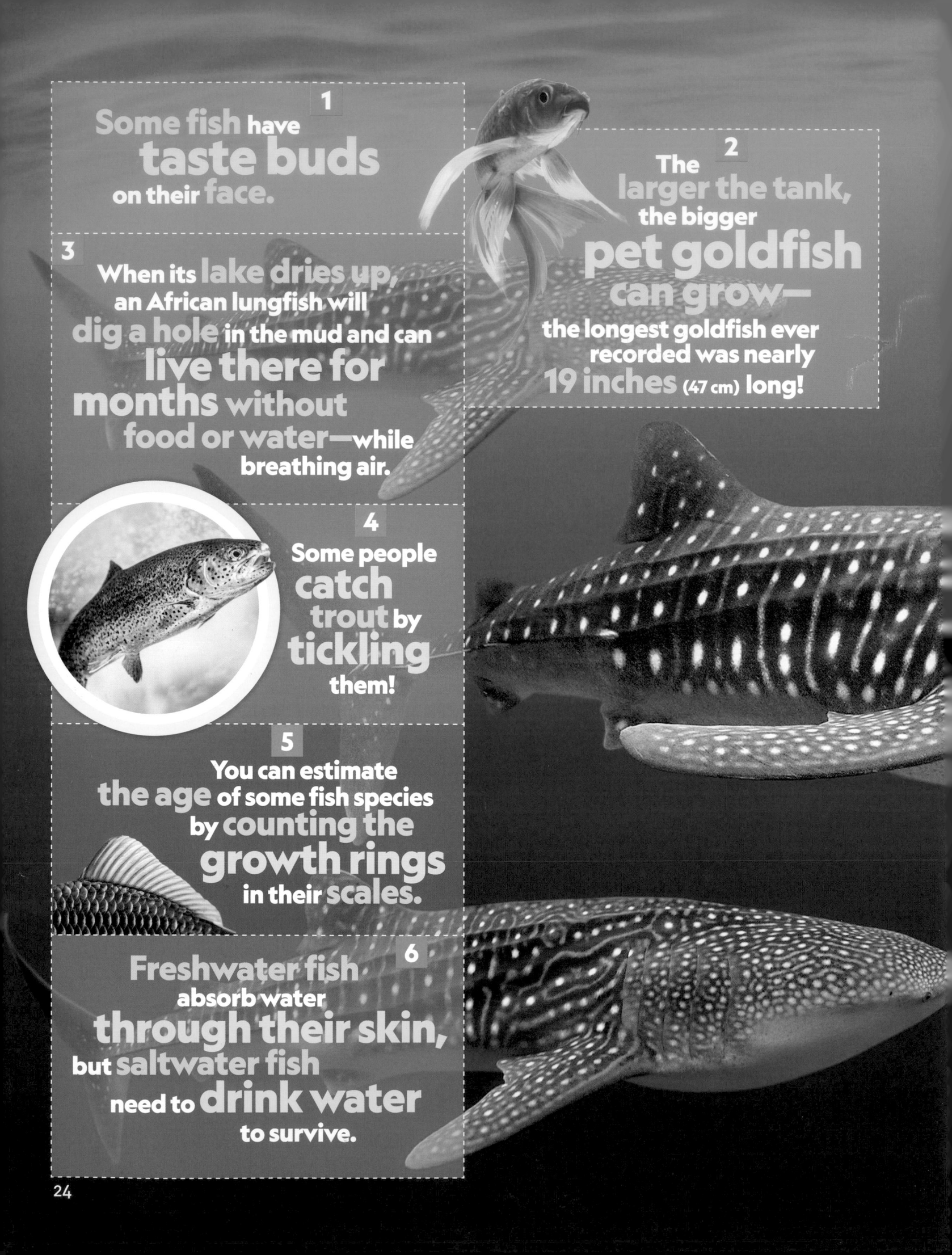

1

Some fish have taste buds on their face.

2

The larger the tank, the bigger pet goldfish can grow—the longest goldfish ever recorded was nearly 19 inches (47 cm) long!

3

When its lake dries up, an African lungfish will dig a hole in the mud and can live there for months without food or water—while breathing air.

4

Some people catch trout by tickling them!

5

You can estimate the age of some fish species by counting the growth rings in their scales.

6

Freshwater fish absorb water through their skin, but saltwater fish need to drink water to survive.

Fishy

Facts to Make You Move Your Fins

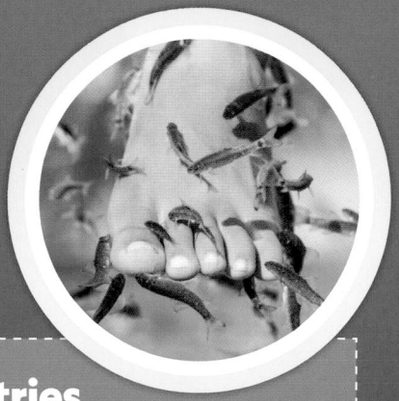

7

In some countries, you can **get a pedicure** in which **tiny fish nibble dead skin** off your feet!

8

The **biggest fish** in the world are **whale sharks,** which can grow **more than 40 feet!** (12 m)

9

The **four-eyed fish** actually has two eyes, each with **two pupils:** The top pupil watches **above the water's surface** for insects and the bottom one looks **down below.**

10

Goldfish can learn tricks! A fantail goldfish named Albert Einstein knew **how to play fetch,** swim through a hoop, and **play football.**

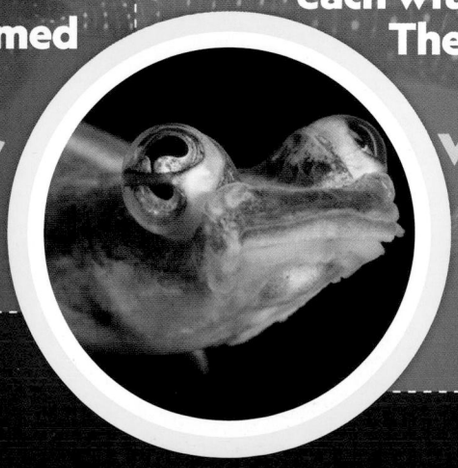

Whale sharks

1

Each one of us has **trillions of viruses inside our bodies** at any given time, even when we're **not sick.**

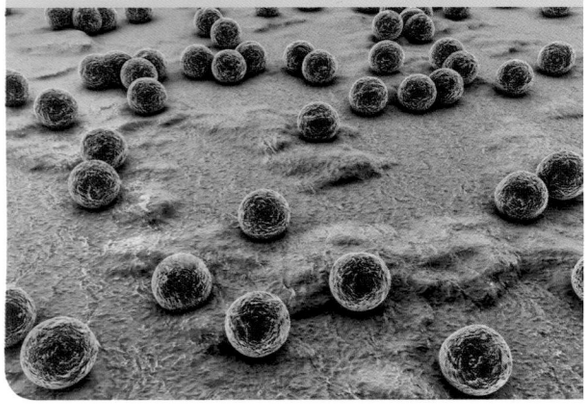

2

There are a **hundred million times** as many **viruses on Earth** as there are **stars** in the universe.

3

Scientists can **create viruses** in a lab.

4

A **sick person** can **spread a virus** up to **six feet** (1.8 m) **away** by sneezing or talking.

5

Millions of common **cold viruses** could fit on the **tip of a pin.**

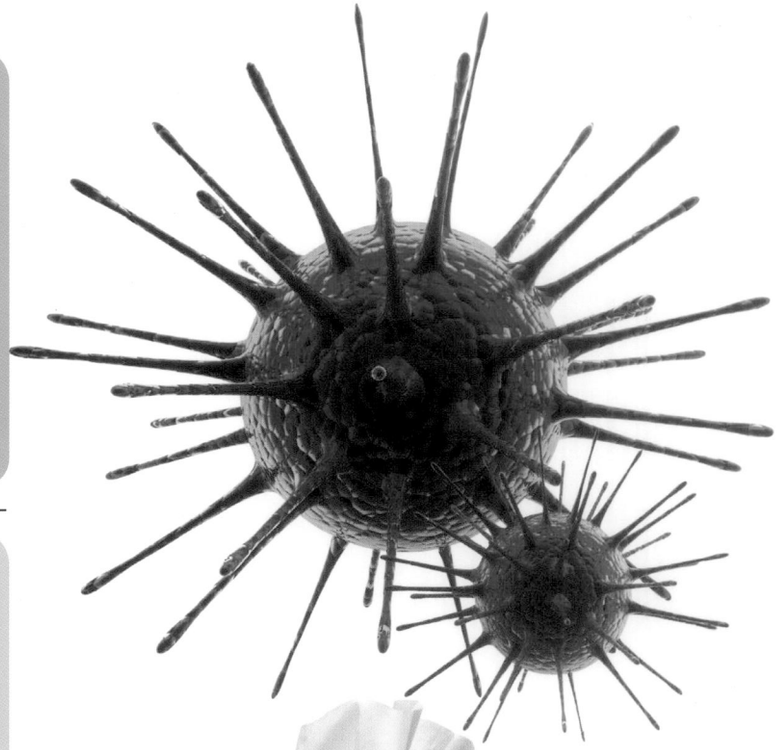

Contagious Facts About Viruses

6

The word "virus" comes from the Latin word for poisonous, slimy liquid.

7

Eating chicken soup has proved to help some people get over a cold faster.

8

Sunlight and specialized laser light can sometimes be used to kill viruses.

9

Scientists are hoping to use viruses to treat acne.

10

Viruses aren't alive, but they aren't dead either.

The blue dragon sea slug uses an air bubble in its stomach to float.

Facts About Birds to Tweet About

1

Birds that fly long distances **lay oval eggs** or eggs with a pointy tip, while birds that fly shorter distances lay **rounder eggs.**

2

Birds **swallow** their food **whole** and then **grind it up** in their **gizzard,** an organ **near the stomach.**

3

There's a village in **Turkey** where people use a **language** made up of **whistles** that sound like **birdsong.**

4

The **tufts** on the **heads of owls** are called **plumicorns.**

5

The **biggest bird of prey known to have existed** was the Haast's eagle. Once found in **New Zealand,** this now extinct raptor **had talons** the size of **tiger claws.**

6

According to **Norse legends,** after eating a **dragon's heart,** a person could understand **bird language.**

7

Some birds practice singing in their **dreams.**

8

Ostriches are the only birds that have **two toes.** Most birds have three or four.

9

Hundreds or thousands of starlings **flying in unison,** swooping and changing direction like a **cloud of smoke,** is called a **murmuration.**

10

Prehistoric birds may have **flown** using **four wings.**

Yellow wagtail

Sparkling Facts About Stuff That Shimmers and Shines

1

Scientists think **our universe** contains at least 100 billion **galaxies,** each with more than **100 billion stars.**

2

The **Black Prince's Ruby,** which is set in the United Kingdom's Imperial State Crown, **isn't actually a ruby at all!** It's a gemstone called a spinel.

3

Diamond Beach in Iceland has black sand and is dotted with chunks of **blue** and **crystal clear ice.**

4

There's a **mosque** in the Middle Eastern country of Oman that contains a **crystal chandelier** that is almost the same size as a **two-story house!**

5

There are **opals** on **Mars.**

6

A company in France makes **lemonade** that contains **flakes** of **real gold.**

7

The **golden mask** of **King Tutankhamun** is covered with stones and glass and weighs **22 pounds** (10 kg).

8

Salt, the **only rock** that **people eat,** was once worth as much as **gold.**

Turn the page for more glittering facts!

9

Some people used to **believe** that **emeralds** could **melt snakes' eyes.**

10

Scientists recently **disproved a belief** that **magpies steal** sparkly objects and **hoard them** in their nests.

11

There once was a Japanese hotel where guests could **take a dip** in a **gold bathtub**— until someone **stole it!**

12

The **golden mole** may be blind, but it has **fur that shimmers** in shades of **blue and green.**

13

The **Hope Diamond,** which is blue, **glows red** if you shine an ultraviolet light on it.

14

The **ancient Maya** decorated their temples with paint made with **crushed mica,** a shimmery rock.

15

Precious metals like gold and platinum may have **come from meteors** that **crashed** into Earth.

16

When disturbed, the **golden tortoise beetle's** shell turns from a **metallic sheen** to a **yellow or red** color with **black spots.**

17

The **world's shiniest living thing** is an African fruit that shimmers like a **blue jewel.**

18

The world's **largest crystals,** found **inside a cave** in Mexico, weigh more than **four school buses** combined.

19

The **mirror spider,** which looks like a tiny **disco ball,** has spots that reflect light, **confusing** predators.

20

The mineral **pyrite,** which is also known as **"fool's gold,"** will **give off sparks** if you **strike it** against something hard.

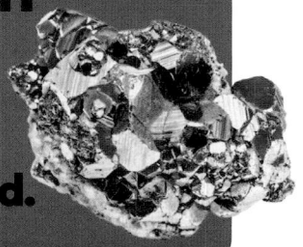

Surprising Facts About Seeds

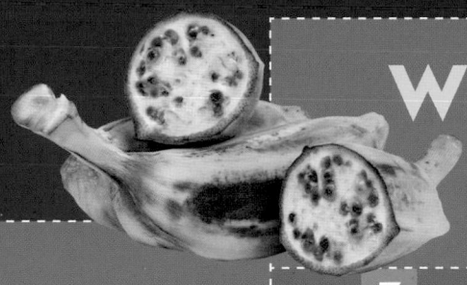

1

Wild bananas have seeds, unlike most farmed bananas.

2

The little **yellow dots** on the outside of a **strawberry** are actually **tiny dry fruits** that contain even **smaller seeds.**

3

The sandbox tree grows small pumpkin-shaped fruits that **explode** and **send seeds flying through the air** nearly 150 feet (46 m) from the tree.

4

The **biggest seed** in the world weighs about as much as a **bulldog!**

5

Scientists are **saving the world's seeds** in a giant **underground freezer,** called a seed vault, in Norway.

6

According to Japanese tradition, certain **cherry seeds** can **guide souls of the dead** back to their family homes.

7

A single **dandelion** plant releases more than **2,000 seeds** each year.

8

Scientists once **grew flowers** from a **32,000-year-old seed.**

9

A type of flowering grass in South Africa has **poop-scented** seeds that **fool dung beetles** into rolling them up and **planting** them in fresh soil.

10

An inventor **created Velcro** after seeing **burrs,** a type of seed, get stuck to his **dog's fur.**

Nifty Facts About Numbers

1

There's a **complex math equation** scientists use to **calculate the chances** that there's other **intelligent life** somewhere in the universe.

2

If **23 people** gather in a group, there's about a **50 percent chance** that at least **two** of them will share the **same birthday.**

3

The average dog is **about as smart** as a **two-year-old** human, can understand **165 words,** and can **count up to 4 or 5.**

4

The first three digits in the number pi (3.14) spell the word "PIE" if you read them backward in a mirror.

5

Omega is a symbol that scientists use to represent how much "stuff" is inside our universe.

6

When a volcano erupted on the island of Krakatoa, in present-day Indonesia, the sound traveled around the planet four times.

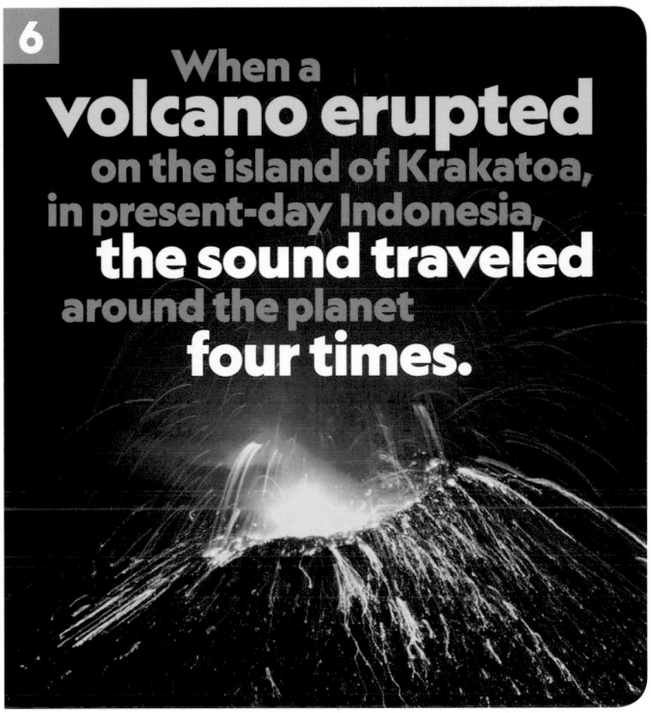

7

Swarms of cicadas—insects found across the northeastern United States—sleep underground and emerge only once every 13 or 17 years.

8

The world's favorite number is 7, according to one study.

9

Albert Einstein's birthday falls on Pi Day—March 14.

10

The person who first used zero as a written symbol originally wrote it as a dot.

Find out what gives this lake its cool colors!

The landscape in Canada's Okanagan Valley looks like a watercolor paint set, with blue, green, and yellow puddles scattered across the ground. But these water spots don't get their color from paint—instead, they're full of minerals left behind as the valley's Spotted Lake evaporates each summer.

WHAT LIES BENEATH

This lake first formed about 10,000 years ago when a glacier melted and created a depression in the ground where the lake now rests. When it rains or snows in the valley, some of the water seeps through fractures in the bedrock, which is the solid rock that sits under the surface soil, and it collects there as groundwater. This is when Spotted Lake's colorful magic happens. The valley's bedrock has a high concentration of minerals called magnesium sulfate, calcium sulfate, and sodium sulfate. As groundwater seeps through the area's bedrock, it absorbs these minerals. The mineralized water then slowly makes its way into the lake when something called hydrostatic pressure occurs. It's sort of like what happens when you try to pour more water on a very wet sponge. The sponge can't hold any more liquid, so some of it leaks out. "Think of Spotted Lake as a bubbling pot of water," geologist Murray Roed says. "The water isn't warm, but it kind of bubbles up all across the lake as the groundwater flows up into the lake."

PASS THE SALT, PLEASE

It's the introduction of these sodium-rich minerals into the lake that gives the spots their unique colors. During the spring, Spotted Lake's water is a murky brown, with the minerals just beginning to settle at the bottom. But by the summertime, most of the lake's water has evaporated. This causes the highly mineralized water that's left over to pool together into spots. The color of each pool depends on the combination of minerals and the reflection of the sun. All of the spots typically contain large amounts of each mineral, which often crystallizes, or hardens. These deposits form walkways that people could possibly stand on when the lake dries out in the late summer.

POWERFUL PUDDLES

Not that walking is recommended. The fish-free lake water is toxic if ingested. Caribou, coyotes, moose, brown bears, and bighorn sheep that live in the Okanagan Valley seem to know it and stay away from the water. Humans, however, have long recognized the healing powers of the lake. Aboriginal Canadians use the lake's mud to help soothe achy joints and other body pains. A strangely patterned body of water, an abundance of local wildlife, and mysterious healing powers? Sounds like Spotted Lake is, well, a spot worth visiting.

Caribou

The mud in Spotted Lake smells like **rotten eggs.**

Spotted Lake has about **400 spots.**

Salt patches on Mars show that the red planet may have once had **spotted lakes!**

Polka Dot Lake

Strange Places

In the **Okanagan** language, this lake is called Klilukt.

There are approximately **two million lakes** in Canada.

1

A medieval sword has **inscriptions** on the blade in a **language** that **no one understands.**

2

A **mail armor** suit was made of up to **30,000 rings** of iron, brass, or steel.

4

Some knights wore **leather armor**, which was made **hard and sturdy** by boiling it in wax or oil.

3

Body armor worn by a **knight's horse** was called barding.

5

A knight's armor was **cleaned with sand and urine** to keep it from **rusting.**

Amazing Facts About Arms & Armor

6 A suit of medieval battle armor weighed less than the typical equipment worn by today's firemen and infantry soldiers.

7 Women, including Joan of Arc, also likely wore armor into battle.

8 A boy who began training at the age of six could become a squire by the age of 14, and a knight when he turned 17 or 18.

9 In the 19th century, warriors in Kiribati, an island nation in the Pacific, wore armor made of coconuts and fish.

10 Blue was a popular color for medieval armor, achieved by heating the metal and then dunking it in water.

1

Sand is actually a **mixture** of **tiny shells, crystals, rocks, and corals** that have broken down over time.

2

The beach area **where waves break** is called the **swash zone.**

3

In the middle of the 1700s, **doctors** started **prescribing visits to the beach** for their **sick patients.**

4

The **white sand** found in some beaches comes from **parrotfish poop**—one large parrotfish can produce **hundreds of pounds** of sand each year!

5

In addition to **white or yellow sand** beaches, some beaches around the world have **green, purple, red, pink,** or **black** sand.

6

Over a third of the world's population lives within **a day's drive** from an **ocean.**

Soak Up These Facts About the Seashore

7

People can **dig their own hot tubs** in the sand at **Hot Water Beach** in New Zealand, where **water wells up** from an underground river that's **heated by the Earth.**

8

Some beaches are made of **"singing sand"** that **hums and squeaks.**

9

A beach can shrink and grow each year as winter waves **pull sand out** into the ocean and summer waves **push the sand back** onto the shore.

10

Sand is used to make **computer chips.**

Shattering Facts About Glass

1 The drawings used to **plan stained-glass** designs are called **cartoons.**

2 **Fiberglass,** a material used in pipes and cars, is made from tiny **threads of glass** that are **woven together.**

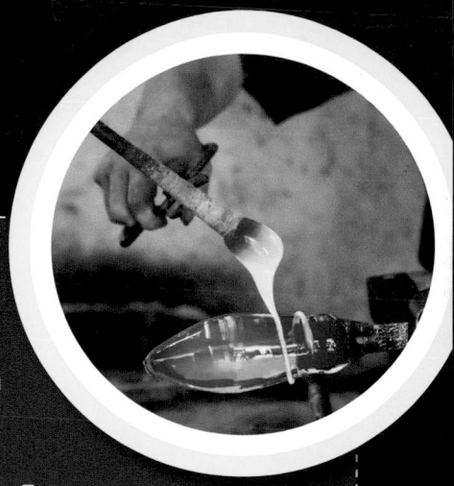

3

Glass is **neither liquid nor solid—** it's something **in between.**

4

Toledo, Ohio, U.S.A., is nicknamed "Glass City" because workers have been **making glass there** for **more than 130 years.**

5

One of the **most valuable glass items** in the world is the Portland Vase, which was said to be made for a **Roman emperor** about 2,000 years ago.

6

Glass that erupts **from volcanoes** is called **obsidian** and is so sharp that **eye surgeons** sometimes use it instead of **steel blades.**

7

Aboard the International Space Station, **scientists** are making a type of **superclear glass** that they hope could be used to build **stronger lasers** and a **faster internet.**

8

Archaeologists have found **pieces of glass** made **by humans** about **3,250 years ago.**

9

Glass can form when **lightning strikes** sand.

10

The first **contact lenses** were **made from glass.**

1

There is a **massive storm** on **Jupiter** that **has lasted** for the past **150 years** and could fit **three Earths** inside it.

2

The TRAPPIST-1 dwarf star, which **has seven Earth-size planets** orbiting it, could be up to **twice as old** as our solar system!

3

Scientists named 60 discoveries of baby moons and clumps of ice and rock after **kitten names: Fluffy, Socks,** and **Whiskers,** to name a few!

4

Saturn's moon Mimas is sometimes referred to as the **Death Star** because its shape resembles the popular ***Star Wars* spacecraft.**

5

On August 21, 1924, there was a national day of **radio silence** so scientists could use a **radio receiver** to listen for **alien signals from Mars.**

6

Some astronauts say **space smells** like **burned steak.**

7

GJ 504b is a **large pink planet** that orbits within a system that scientists estimate is about **160 million years old.**

8

The Boomerang Nebula is the **coldest known object** in the universe at **nearly minus 460°F** (-270°C).

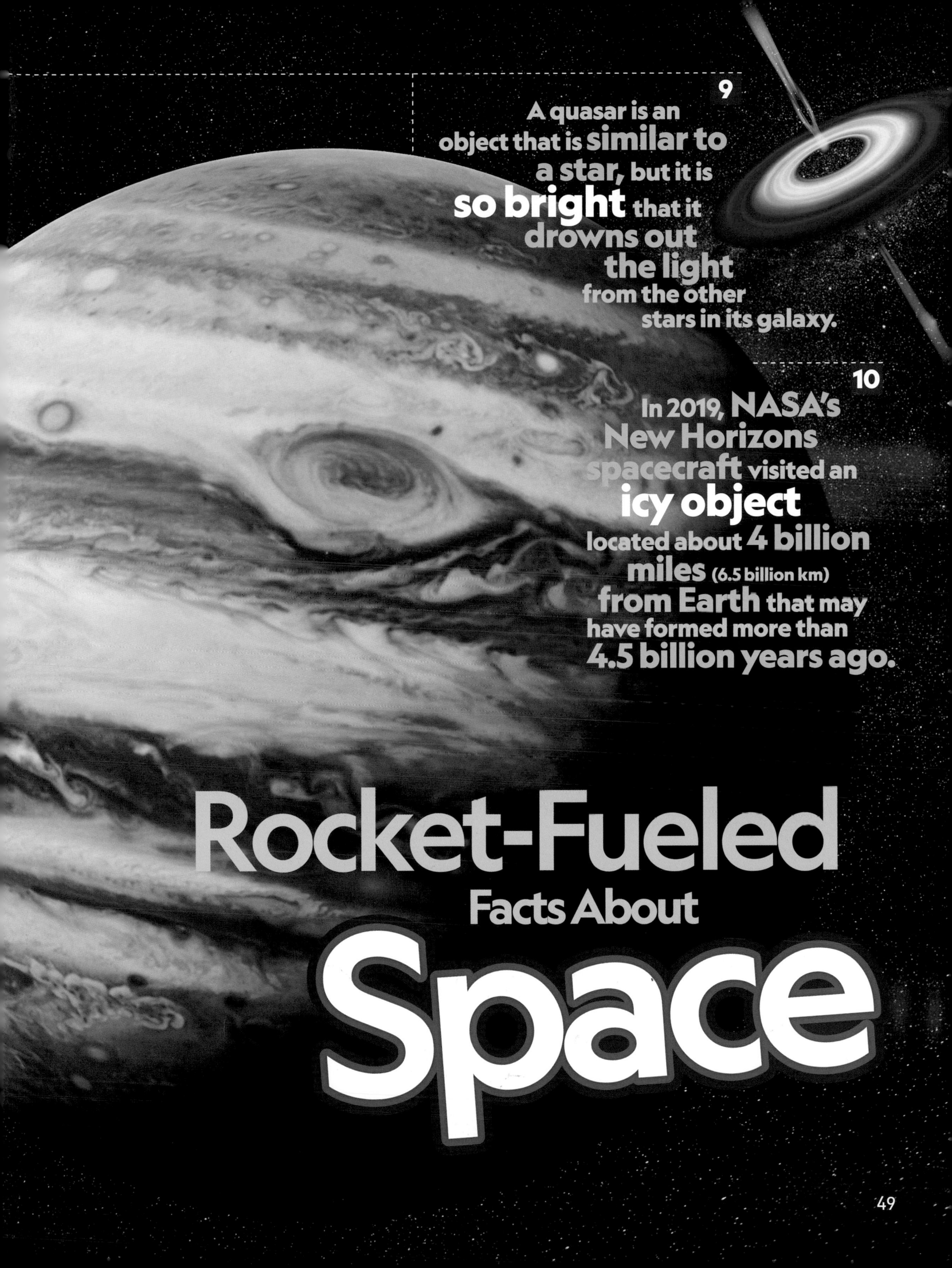

9

A quasar is an object that is **similar to a star,** but it is **so bright** that it **drowns out the light** from the other stars in its galaxy.

10

In 2019, **NASA's New Horizons spacecraft** visited an **icy object** located about **4 billion miles** (6.5 billion km) **from Earth** that may have formed more than **4.5 billion years ago.**

Rocket-Fueled Facts About Space

1

Cinnabar is one of the most toxic minerals on Earth—it's often referred to as "dragon's blood."

2

The sandstone in Vermilion Cliffs National Monument in Arizona, U.S.A., appears to change color throughout the day.

3

The first lasers were made from artificial ruby crystals.

4

Scientists believe that in billions of years, the sun will become one huge diamond.

5

"Garnet" comes from a Latin word that translates to "pomegranate."

Facts That Totally Rock

6

Tourmaline is also known as the **"rainbow gem"** because it comes in **every color!**

7

A group of over 1,500 **limestone mounds** in the Philippines are called the **Chocolate Hills.**

8

More than **50,000 people** a year head to Emerald Hollow Mine in North Carolina, U.S.A., to **dig for emeralds.** Finders keepers!

9

The **skinny rock formations** left over from **volcanic eruptions** in Göreme National Park in Turkey are known as **"fairy chimneys."**

10

Endoliths are tiny living organisms that **live inside rocks,** giving a whole new meaning to the idea of a **pet rock.**

Ultrahot Facts About Fire

1

Sometimes wildfires form their own tornadoes, called **firenados.**

2

Fire isn't an object— it's an event caused by a chemical reaction in a mixture of gases.

3

Fires with **more oxygen** are blue and burn the hottest; fires with **less oxygen** are yellow and burn the coolest.

4

Wildfires can create their own storm clouds, called flammagenitus or pyrocumulus clouds.

5

The chemicals in pistachios **give off heat,** so if too many of the nuts are packaged together they can actually burst into flames.

6

The remains of the oldest known **campfire** are about one million years old.

7

Earth is the only **known planet** in our solar system where fire occurs.

8

The **Olympic torch** is lit with a curved mirror that focuses the sun's rays into a **superhot beam.**

9

A coal fire under a mountain in Australia has been burning continuously for **6,000 years.**

10

Fireworks get their colors from chemicals: Strontium and lithium burn red, calcium burns orange, sodium burns yellow, barium burns green, and copper burns blue.

FLOATING UMBRELLAS

WHAT Umbrella art

WHERE Águeda, Portugal

DETAILS Paging Mary Poppins! As part of an art festival called AgitÁgueda, hundreds of parasols were seen floating above this Portuguese street. Though they looked like they were suspended in midair, the umbrellas were actually held in place by wires connected to buildings on both sides of the street. Nothing's going to rain on this artistic parade.

Extreme Weirdness

ICE CUBE ON WHEELS

WHAT Truck made of ice

WHERE Hensall, Canada

DETAILS It's going to be an icy ride. This functional truck has a body made of more than 11,000 pounds (nearly 5,000 kg) of ice. Built over a base frame with wheels, the icy exterior covers a real engine, brakes, and steering wheel. It runs on a battery that's specially designed to start in frigid conditions that would keep most cars from revving up. The car can only go short distances—but what a great place to chill!

SEA CREATURES ROCK OUT

WHAT Underwater band

WHERE Beijing, China

DETAILS Talk about making a splash! Musicians wearing marine animal costumes grooved inside a giant, water-filled tank at the Beijing Aquarium to celebrate the Chinese New Year. Billed as the country's first underwater band, they entertained the visitors—and maybe the fish, too.

RUNNING OF THE APES

WHAT Great Gorilla Run

WHERE London, England

DETAILS On your mark, get set, go-rilla! Over a thousand runners put on furry costumes to run across London's Tower Bridge as part of the Great Gorilla Run. The annual event raises money to help save the primate species from extinction. Now that's a cause to go ape for.

UNDERWATER DINING

WHAT Aquarium-dining divers

WHERE London, England

DETAILS There's seafood and then there's undersea-food. Divers at a London aquarium enjoyed an underwater fish supper with a green sea turtle to promote sustainable fishing practices. Their goal was to encourage the protection of overfished marine life such as Atlantic salmon. Looks like the event went swimmingly.

KERMIT SALUTES STATUE

WHAT Mexico City's summer celebration

WHERE Mexico City, Mexico

DETAILS It's easy being green when you're the star of the parade. A giant Kermit the Frog balloon floated by the capital's famous Angel of Independence monument as part of a parade to welcome summer. The Muppet was joined by the likes of Mickey Mouse and Spider-Man. Who knew frogs could fly?

Smooth Facts About Silk

1

According to Chinese legends, silk was first discovered when a silkworm cocoon fell into the empress's cup of tea and unraveled to reveal a single thread.

2

Spider silk is so strong that it's often compared to steel.

3

The thread in a silkworm cocoon can be up to a mile long. (1.6 km)

4

Some types of crickets can make silk.

5

Some Vikings used silk to decorate their burial ships.

6

Golden orb weaving spiders spin yellow silk.

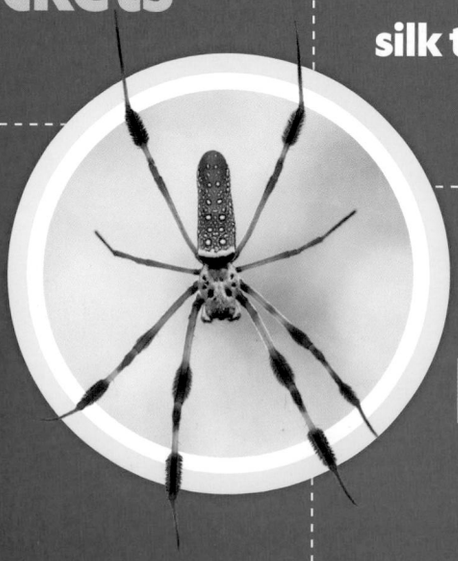

7

Researchers have discovered prehistoric silk in 8,500-year-old tombs.

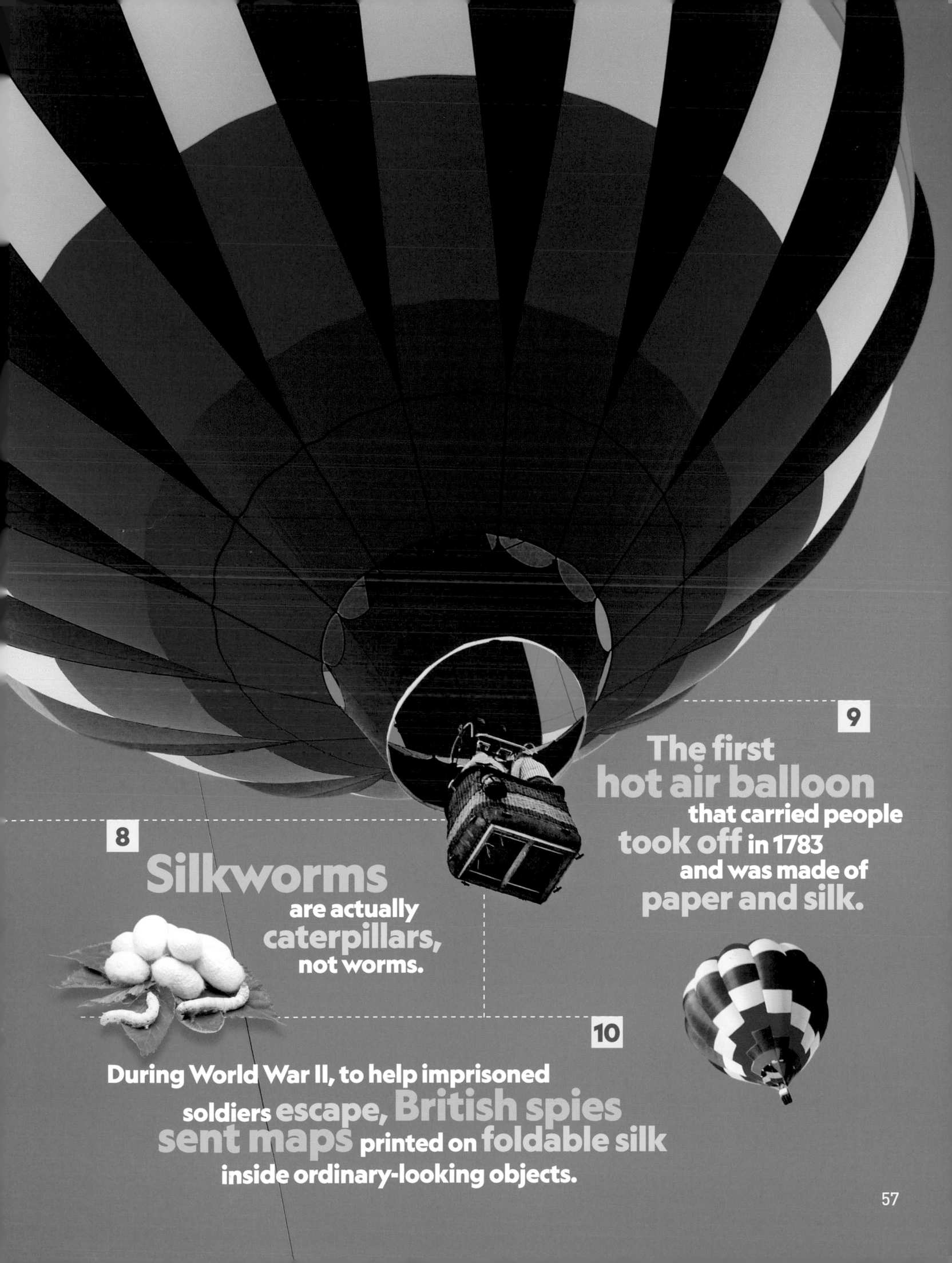

9

The first **hot air balloon** that carried people **took off** in 1783 and was made of **paper and silk.**

8

Silkworms are actually **caterpillars,** not worms.

10

During World War II, to help imprisoned soldiers **escape, British spies sent maps** printed on **foldable silk** inside ordinary-looking objects.

Sugar-Coated Facts About Candy

1

The **lollipop** is said to be named after a **racing horse** named **Lolly Pop.**

2

There are **lightning bug gummy** candies that actually **light up** when squeezed.

3

In 1969, the astronauts of the **Apollo 9** space mission **nicknamed** one module of their spacecraft **Gumdrop.**

4

Gum chewing may improve **test scores.**

5

The largest **bubble-gum bubble** ever recorded to date was **20 inches** (51 cm) in diameter—that's twice the diameter of a **basketball!**

6

Salsagheti is a **sweet and spicy** spaghetti-like gummy candy that **comes with a sauce** to pour over the **"noodles."**

8

The **first bubblegum,** made in 1906, was called **Blibber-Blubber.**

7

You can buy **wasabi-flavored Kit Kat bars** in Japan.

9

There's a **marshmallow festival** in Indiana, U.S.A., every year, with **games,** a marshmallow **bake-off,** and a pizza-eating contest with **marshmallow toppings!**

Turn the page for more sweet candy facts!

10

Salt Lake City, Utah, U.S.A., **eats the most Jell-O** of any city in the **entire world.**

11

Candy didn't become a part of celebrating **Halloween** until **the 1950s.**

12

The word **"sweetmeats,"** used in the United Kingdom, refers to treats **made of sugar** or **covered in sugar.**

13

At **U.S. president Ronald Reagan's** inauguration, attendees ate more than three tons (2.7 t) of **red, white, and blue jelly beans.**

14

The man who **invented cotton candy** was a **dentist.**

15

Germans eat more candy on average than citizens from **any other country.**

16

Tootsie Rolls were added to **soldiers' rations** during World War II because they **didn't melt.**

17

A **5,000-year-old** piece of **chewing gum** was discovered in Finland!

18

Enough **candy corn** is made every year to give **every person on Earth** one kernel.

19

According to a survey, most people **eat the ears** off of their chocolate **Easter bunnies** **before** they eat **anything else.**

20

Fashion stylists once **made a dress** out of **50,000 gummy bears**—it weighed **220 pounds!** (100 kg)

1

The **Southern Cross** constellation appears on **Brazilian coins.**

2

Scientists found a **32,000-year-old** carving on an **ivory tablet** of an object that could represent the **Orion constellation.**

3

Most of the names for today's **constellations** came from the **ancient Greeks.**

4

The **Big Dipper** is **not actually a constellation** but an **asterism,** a group of stars that are part of a **larger constellation.**

5

The **North Star** is **the brightest star** in the constellation **Ursa Minor,** also known as the **Little Bear.**

6

There are **88 constellations** visible in **Earth's sky.**

Cosmic

Facts About Constellations

7

The **largest constellation** is **Hydra,** which is in the **shape of a water snake.**

8

Some experts believe that the **ancient Egyptians** used the position of the **constellations** to decide **where to build** their temples and monuments.

9

The **Chinese zodiac** calendar may be based on the **path of Jupiter** as it crosses different **constellations** during the year.

10

The **brightest star** in the constellation **Leo** is actually made up of **four separate stars.**

Pizza

Facts By the Slice

1

A **rooftop pizzeria** in Cuba delivers its pies by **lowering them in baskets** to customers **waiting on the sidewalk** below.

2

Italy passed a law requiring that any Margherita pizza must use **specific types** of **flour, yeast, and cheese,** and the dough must be **kneaded by hand.**

3

Ancient Greeks made the **first food to resemble pizza**—a circle of bread with toppings, but no tomato sauce.

4

In the United States, **National Pizza Day** is on February 9.

5

In Scotland, pizza is sometimes dipped in batter and **deep-fried.**

6

Las Vegas, Nevada, U.S.A., hosts an annual **Pizza Convention** where competitors juggle spinning pizza dough discs while dancing to music.

8

Because of the tomato sauce, a slice of pizza counts as a **serving of vegetables** in school lunches in the United States.

7

The **most expensive pizza** is made with black squid ink dough, truffle oil, caviar, Stilton cheese, and edible gold flakes.

9

The **biggest pizza** ever made was 2.5 times as big as a basketball court.

10

Pac-Man's shape was inspired by a whole pizza with a slice removed.

Cool Facts About Copycats

1

Cuttlefish sometimes imitate hermit crabs to sneak up on fish and to look less appetizing to predators.

2

Opossums play dead and give off a special rotting scent to trick predators into walking away.

3

Bee orchids have petals that look like bees to attract pollinators.

4

To scare off enemies, burrowing owl chicks give off a rattling hiss similar to that of rattlesnakes.

5

Blue jays can scream like hawks.

6

An insect called the female orchid mantis **pretends to be a flower** to catch prey.

7

California ground squirrels chew up rattlesnake skins and **cover themselves in the goo** to hide their natural scent.

8

In the Amazon jungle, margay cats lure prey by copying the call of monkeys they like to eat.

9

Dogs can mimic some human gestures.

10

The lithops plant **blends in** with its environment by looking like a rock.

What's the Difference?

Check out these similar pairings and see how you can determine this from that!

CRAYFISH VS. LOBSTER

Crayfish might look like small lobsters, but there's more to each of these creatures than meets the eye. These pinchy critters are both arthropods, which means that they wear their skeletons on the outside of their bodies, as do crabs, shrimp, and their land-dwelling counterparts, insects and arachnids. Lobsters and crayfish look similar, too: They both have five pairs of legs, five pairs of tiny limbs called swimmerets, and one pair of larger claws, including one claw for cutting and the other for crushing. However, lobsters are big and live in salt water, while crayfish are small and live in freshwater lakes, streams, rivers, and ponds. Crayfish also build water-filled underground tunnels during the fall and winter seasons, whereas lobsters spend their time on the ocean floor. Whether you find yourself face to face with a crayfish or a lobster, keep your hands away from their claws!

VITAMIN VS. MINERAL

We get both of these in our food, and we find them in gummy vitamin supplements. But what is the difference between a vitamin and a mineral? And why do we need them at all? The answer is that, apart from vitamin D, these supplements contain molecules your body cannot make on its own. Vitamins are made by plants and other animals. Some of these dissolve in fat, which means your body can store them, but others dissolve in water, which means that anything you don't use gets washed out when you pee, so you need to replace these vitamins every day. Minerals, however, are elements that come from rocks and soil and get absorbed by plants, which then pass minerals up the food chain. Some animals, like goats, get minerals by chewing rocks and licking salt. Thankfully, humans only need to spend some time in the sun, eat healthy foods, and take the occasional gummy supplement to get these nutrients!

TOAD VS. FROG

They may look a lot alike and have one happy hop, but frogs and toads are different characters. If you're in doubt about what to call one of these amphibians, stick with "frog," since that broad category includes all toads. Otherwise, the rule of thumb for distinguishing between the two is this: Frogs hop on long legs and have smooth, wet-looking skin. Toads are a subcategory of frogs that crawl on short legs and have dry, bumpy skin. Frogs are more likely to be seen in moist habitats. Toads are more likely to be seen in dry habitats. With so many differences, can frogs and toads in nature really be friends? Unfortunately, in nature you are more likely to see them hunting each other than to see them sharing a friendly swim!

SEAL VS. SEA LION VS. SEA OTTER

There are a few things that set these three adorable, brown, furry swimmers apart. Seals and sea lions belong to a group called pinnipeds, meaning "fin foot." Pinnipeds have a thick layer of blubber under their furry skin to stay warm. One of the most obvious differences between them is the size and position of their flippers. Sea lions are covered in skin and have long flippers that they use to lift themselves off the ground to "walk." Seals, on the other hand, are covered in fur and have short flippers that can't lift the seal's body, so seals move on the ground like caterpillars. Sea lions also have visible earflaps, but seals do not. When it comes to sea otters, they belong to the same group as weasels, have paws rather than flippers, and stay warm under a thick fur coat.

NOCTURNAL VS. CREPUSCULAR

There are lots of reasons to sleep during the day if you're a nocturnal animal. It's usually cooler at night, which is important if you live in a place that gets very hot or very dry. Small nocturnal mammals also forage or hunt for food because the cover of darkness makes it harder for predators to see them. Badgers, bats, fennec foxes, and sloths that are active at night are nocturnal, and their eyes are especially good at seeing in dim light. But midnight shenanigans aren't a good fit for everyone. Creatures like cats, deer, opossums, and fireflies can do well by hunting and socializing during crepuscule, which is just before sunrise or sunset. At this time of day, fewer predators may be about, and the foods they prefer are easier to snatch.

Sea lions

Radiant Facts About Rainbows

1

Scientists used a laser to create a **repeating rainbow**—resulting in 200 rainbows **stacked on top** of one another.

2

There's a **mountain in Peru** that has **rainbow-colored stripes.**

3

The order of colors in a rainbow is **always red on top** and violet on the bottom, **unless it's a double rainbow,** in which case the colors of the second rainbow **are flipped.**

4

Scientists think there **might be rainbows** on **Saturn's moon Titan.**

5

Triple and quadruple rainbows exist in nature.

6

A rainbow actually has 100 million colors, but most people can only see one million different colors.

7

It's almost impossible to see a full rainbow in the sky at noon.

8

Rainbows have no end—they are circles.

9

If you look out the window of an airplane, sometimes you can see rainbow rings, called "glories," on the surface of clouds.

10

Rainbows are even wider than what we can see. There are certain wavelengths we can't see as color that extend beyond the red and violet bands.

Dazzling Facts About Deserts

1 Desert-dwelling **fennec foxes** never have to drink water.

2 **Tumbleweeds,** a common desert plant, are originally from Russia.

3

Deserts aren't always hot—temperatures in Mongolia's Gobi can drop to nearly -29°F (-34°C)—almost as cold as winter temperatures on Mount Everest.

4

Deserts that get unusually heavy rainfall sometimes experience a "super bloom" of flowers that open almost overnight.

5

Satellite pictures show that there used to be an enormous river flowing through the Sahara desert.

6

Any place that gets less than 10 inches (25 cm) of rain each year is considered a desert.

7

Some parts of Chile's Atacama Desert have never had recorded rainfall.

8

The Gobi is growing bigger each year. In China, they've planted a "Great Green Wall"—more than 66 billion trees—to hold the desert back.

9

Deserts cover more than one-fifth of our planet's surface.

10

A large field of sand dunes is called an erg.

Facts About Lava to Warm Up To

1

When lava flows fast, it hardens into rough, **craggy chunks** called aa. When lava flows slowly, it forms **smooth rolls** and shiny coils called **pahoehoe.**

2

Lava **temperatures** can range from **1300 to 2300°F** (700 to 1250°C).

3

It's considered **bad luck** to **remove lava rocks** from the Hawaiian Islands.

4

Below Earth's crust, there are **giant blobs** of mysterious **molten metal** that rise and sink like a super slow **lava lamp.**

5

Half-pipes have been **carved by lava flows** at a ski resort near an **active volcano** in Chile.

6

People use **pumice stones** to **scrub off dead skin** from their bodies, but these special stones are actually **pieces of lava** that erupted underwater and **floated to the surface.**

7

There's a volcano in Tanzania, Africa, that spews a **rare type of lava** that **turns silver when it cools.**

8

Sometimes when small drops of liquid lava are **blown by the wind,** they transform into **golden threads** known as **Pele's hair.**

9

Half of CoRoT-7b—a planet **489 light-years** away from Earth—is covered with an **ocean of lava.**

10

Lava is the term for **magma** (molten rock) that **reaches the surface of the planet.**

Scaly Facts About Reptiles

1

Pink iguanas live on an island in **the Galápagos.**

2

In the Florida Everglades, U.S.A., pet **Burmese pythons** released into the wild **can grow so big** that they constrict and **eat alligators.**

3

Some snakes are able to **glide through the air** between tree branches, almost as if they're **flying!**

4

A **crocodile** grows up to **3,000 teeth** in its lifetime.

5

Basilisk lizards can run on the surface of water.

6

Anole lizards do push-ups as a warning to other lizards.

7

A chameleon's tongue can shoot out of its mouth and grab an insect faster than you can blink your eyes.

8

Ancient snakes had legs! Today's pythons and boa constrictors have tiny leg bones in the muscles near their tails.

9

A turtle's shell is covered in bony plates called scutes, which are made of the same material as human fingernails.

10

Scientists are studying Komodo dragon blood to possibly make medicine for humans.

1 The United States military **fed soldiers** peanut butter and jelly sandwiches **during World War II.**

2 College students in Philadelphia, Pennsylvania, U.S.A., set a **world record** by making **49,100** peanut butter and jelly sandwiches **in one hour.**

3 **In space, astronauts** make peanut butter and jelly sandwiches with **tortillas,** using **tape** and **Velcro** to hold supplies down.

4 **April 2** is **National Peanut Butter and Jelly** Day in the United States.

5 The **world's largest** PB&J sandwich **weighed** nearly as much as a **large male polar bear.**

6 The average **American eats 1,500** PB&J sandwiches **before they graduate** high school.

7

Peanut butter used to be served on sandwiches with **pimento cheese,** celery, cucumbers, and **edible flowers.**

8

The **first recorded recipe** for **PB&J** was published in a cookbook **in 1901.**

9

In the early 1900s, **peanut butter sandwiches** were served to **wealthy people.**

10

A favorite **pregame snack** of many **pro basketball players** is a PB&J sandwich.

Finger-Licking Facts About Peanut Butter and Jelly

1

Butterflies **hide** under leaves or mushrooms **when it rains.**

2

If the outside temperature is **below 60°F** (16°C), butterflies must **warm their wings** in the sun **before flying.**

3

A **group** of butterflies is sometimes **called a flutter.**

4

Blue morpho butterflies aren't actually blue. Their wings have **tiny prisms** that reflect light, making them **appear blue.**

5

Butterflies live on **every continent** of the world **except Antarctica.**

6

Butterflies **taste** with **their feet.**

7

Butterflies **can remember** things they **learned as caterpillars,** even though their **brains turn to goo** during metamorphosis.

8

Some caterpillars **can disguise** themselves **as ants.**

9

Butterflies suck up the **nutrients they need** from **moist dirt, dead animals,** and **even poop,** a behavior called mud puddling.

Fluttering Facts About Butterflies

10

Some butterflies have ears on their wings.

Checkered swallowtail

Dreamy Facts to Sleep On

1

Some people **dream** in **black and white.**

2

Some scientists **believe** that **babies start to dream before they're born.**

3

The invention of the **sewing machine, Google,** and Einstein's **theory of relativity** were all ideas **inspired by dreams.**

4

Our brains can **solve complex problems—** like how to fix something, or how to handle a disagreement with someone— **while we're dreaming.**

5

Dreaming can **improve** your memory.

6

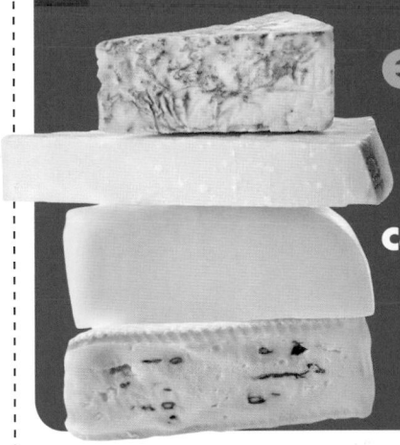

According to one study, **eating cheese** before bed can cause people to have **weird dreams.**

Most people **dream** at least **four to six** times a night.

8

7

Some people are **able to control** what happens in **their dreams.** This type of dreaming is called lucid dreaming or **"dream yoga."**

People who **wake up** during a **dream** are more likely to **remember it.**

9

10

Surveys show that some of the **most common dreams** are about **falling, being chased,** teachers or school situations, and **flying.**

Frigid Facts About the Arctic

1

Every year around **December 21**, the night in the Arctic Circle is so long there's **no sunrise**, and around **June 21**, the day is so long there's **no sunset**.

2

Some dinosaurs lived in the Arctic.

3

One **extra-furry** species of **bumblebee** survives in the Arctic by **shivering** to stay warm.

4

Eight nations have territory in the **Arctic Circle:** Canada, Russia, the United States, Iceland, Greenland, Norway, Finland, and Sweden.

5

Clouds created by **rising gas** from **bird poop** may help to **keep the Arctic cool.**

Polar bear

6

The **average winter temperature** in the Arctic is about **minus 40°F** (-40°C).

7

The name **"Arctic"** comes from the **Greek word** for **bear,** *arktos.*

8

The **Arctic Ocean** is the **shallowest ocean** on Earth.

9

Arctic terns fly more than **a million miles** (1.6 million km) in their lifetimes—that's the same distance as making **three round-trip** flights to **the moon.**

10

If you hold **a compass** while standing directly over the **magnetic North Pole,** the arrow will **stop working, spin randomly,** or point to something magnetic on **your body.**

Walt Disney
modeled Sleeping
Beauty's castle
after
Neuschwanstein
Castle in
Germany.

1

Photos of a **galloping horse,** showing that its **feet are off the ground** mid-stride, were an inspiration for the **invention of movies** in the late 1800s.

2

The **first popular camera** sold to everyday consumers was called the Kodak Brownie, and it **cost only $1!**

3

The **first photograph**—taken in 1826—was black and white and took **several hours to develop.**

4

Astronauts left **12 cameras** behind on the surface of **the moon** to **save weight** on the trip back to Earth.

5

The **first photograph** was called a **"sun drawing."**

6

During the 1800s, Great Britain's **Queen Victoria** was a huge **fan of photography.** She learned to develop her own pictures and had a private **darkroom** built in **Buckingham Palace.**

Picture

These Facts About Photography

7 A chemist named Robert Cornelius took his own picture—the first selfie—in 1839.

8 Patrick Peterson, a professional football player, holds the world record for most selfies taken in an hour: 1,449!

9 World Photo Day is August 19.

10 Over one billion photos are shared on social media every day.

1

Mucus, snot, mucilage, ectoplasm, and **gloop** are all names for **slime.**

2

Velvet worms **shoot slime** out of the sides of their heads to **trap their prey.**

3

Maggot slime can be used to help **heal wounds.**

4

Snail slime is added to some products used to **soften skin.**

Squishy Facts About Slime

5

If a predator attacks, a **hagfish** will release **gallons of slime** to attempt to **choke the attacker.**

6

Parrotfish **sleep in a bubble** of **mucus** at night.

7

The **yellow slime mold** *Fuligo septica* is often called **"scrambled egg"** or **"dog vomit"** slime mold.

8

Government researchers once developed a **"sticky foam gun"** that would **stop criminals** by **shooting slime.**

9

The **human body** can **make enough mucus** every day to fill an **ostrich egg.**

10

Sea creatures called larvaceans **build a slimy "house"** around themselves **to catch** microscopic **bits of food** in the water.

Outrageous Facts About Everything Under Our Feet

1 Soil is more than just dirt—it includes so many microbes and bugs that some scientists actually say it's alive.

2 Scientists estimate that more than a quarter of all living species can be found in soils.

3 You won't sink underground if you step in quicksand—humans will only sink up to their waist.

4

Disney World is built over a **network of tunnels,** commonly called a **utilidor.**

5

There's one **ant colony** that has built vast **underground cities** on **every continent** except Antarctica.

6

There could be a **massive body of water** that lies deep below Earth's surface—a body **three times** larger than all Earth's **oceans put together.**

7

Rivers that used to be aboveground now flow **underneath New York City.**

8

You can ride an **underground Ferris wheel** in Romania.

9

Police found an **abandoned movie theater** in the **catacombs** underneath Paris, where miles of tunnels are lined with **skulls and bones.**

10

Elephants send low-frequency **vibration messages** to each other **through the ground.**

Razor-Sharp Towers Hide a Wild World

A forbidding forest of pointed peaks soars above the surrounding jungle landscape. This surreal limestone lair looks like a challenge straight out of a video game. The eye-popping spot—called Tsingy de Bemaraha national park and reserve—is located in western Madagascar, an island off the southeast coast of Africa.

It's easy to see why the word "tsingy" (pronounced sing-EE) means "where one cannot walk barefoot" in the local Malagasy language. But in this brutal landscape, many creatures make their home among these stone towers where only a few humans dare to set foot.

Von der Decken's sifakas

One **species of gecko** in Madagascar looks like a **dead leaf.**

The **aye-aye lemur** was once thought to be **extinct.**

90% of the species found in Madagascar are found **nowhere else** on Earth.

WATER AT WORK

Around 200 million years ago, the limestone plateau that makes up Tsingy de Bemaraha was part of the seabed. Over millions of years, the limestone layers below the water slowly rose above the sea level. Heavy rains continually sculpted the land, altering its shape. "When rainwater flows into cracks in the landscape, it dissolves the rock," says Márton Veress, a geomorphologist (someone who studies the evolution of the Earth's surface). The constant dissolution created crevasses, or deep open cracks, across the top layer of land. Over time, the tops of the rocks sharpened into the knife-like points visible today.

CREATURE FEATURES

You won't find many humans venturing among those spiky limestone towers—just a few locals, plus some brave scientists and tourists with rugged rock-climbing gear. But you'll spot plenty of animals in the park. "The biodiversity of Tsingy de Bemaraha is unique even when compared to the rest of Madagascar, which hosts many animals found nowhere else on the planet," primatologist Travis Steffens says. "The tsingy is like its own separate island within an island." That's because the wildlife of Tsingy de Bemaraha had to adapt to the park's challenging surroundings, learning to survive everywhere from large dry forests to dense jungle-like tropical areas that sprouted up through crevasses in the landscape. Lemurs in particular thrive in the tsingy—11 species call it home. Six of those species are endangered. Among them is the white-furred Von der Decken's sifaka, which developed powerful hind legs to leap up to 30 feet (9 m) from peak to peak. Its hands have developed soft pads that allow it to grip the rocks as it clings vertically and leaps across the park's spikes. Even the plants have adapted to life in the unusual tsingy. For example, xerophytes (pronounced ZEE-roh-fites) found in the tsingy's dry forests can stretch their long, rope-like roots into various parts of the rock face in search of water.

MORE TO EXPLORE

There's still so much to uncover in this strange and stunning no-man's-land, and scientists continue to encounter new plant and animal species as they study the park. Who knows what new discoveries await those brave enough to venture into Tsingy de Bemaraha's treacherous terrain?

Stone Forest

Strange Places

Madagascar is home to **baobab trees** more than **1,000 years old.**

Dancing lemurs can't walk on all fours—they **hop sideways.**

Facts About Fur, Feathers, Skin, and Scales

1 You shed your entire outer layer of skin about once a month.

2 Flamingos are born with gray or white feathers that turn pink over time because of the algae and shrimp the birds eat.

3 Some geckos and lizards eat their skin after they shed it.

4

Special **jagged feathers** on **owls' wings** help muffle noise, allowing them to fly **almost silently.**

5

A square inch (6.5 sq cm) of **human skin** contains about 1,000 **nerve endings.**

6

Chameleons can **change their color** because of special **light-reflecting crystals** in their skin.

7

Dogs are born with **fuzzy fur** known as a **puppy coat,** which is replaced by a thicker **adult coat** within a few months.

8

The **ancient Maya** used the bright green and blue feathers of the **quetzal** bird as **currency.**

9

Some people are born with **blue skin.**

Turn the page for more cool facts on coverings!

10

Baby dolphins are born with **whiskers** on their chins.

11

Fish scales are an ingredient **used in some lipsticks.**

12

Hippos are protected from **sunburn** by a sticky orange and red oil **they secrete from sweat glands** all over their skin.

13

Any animal that has **bare skin**—humans, whales, even cats and dogs (on their noses)—**can get sunburned.**

14

Some people are born **without fingerprints.**

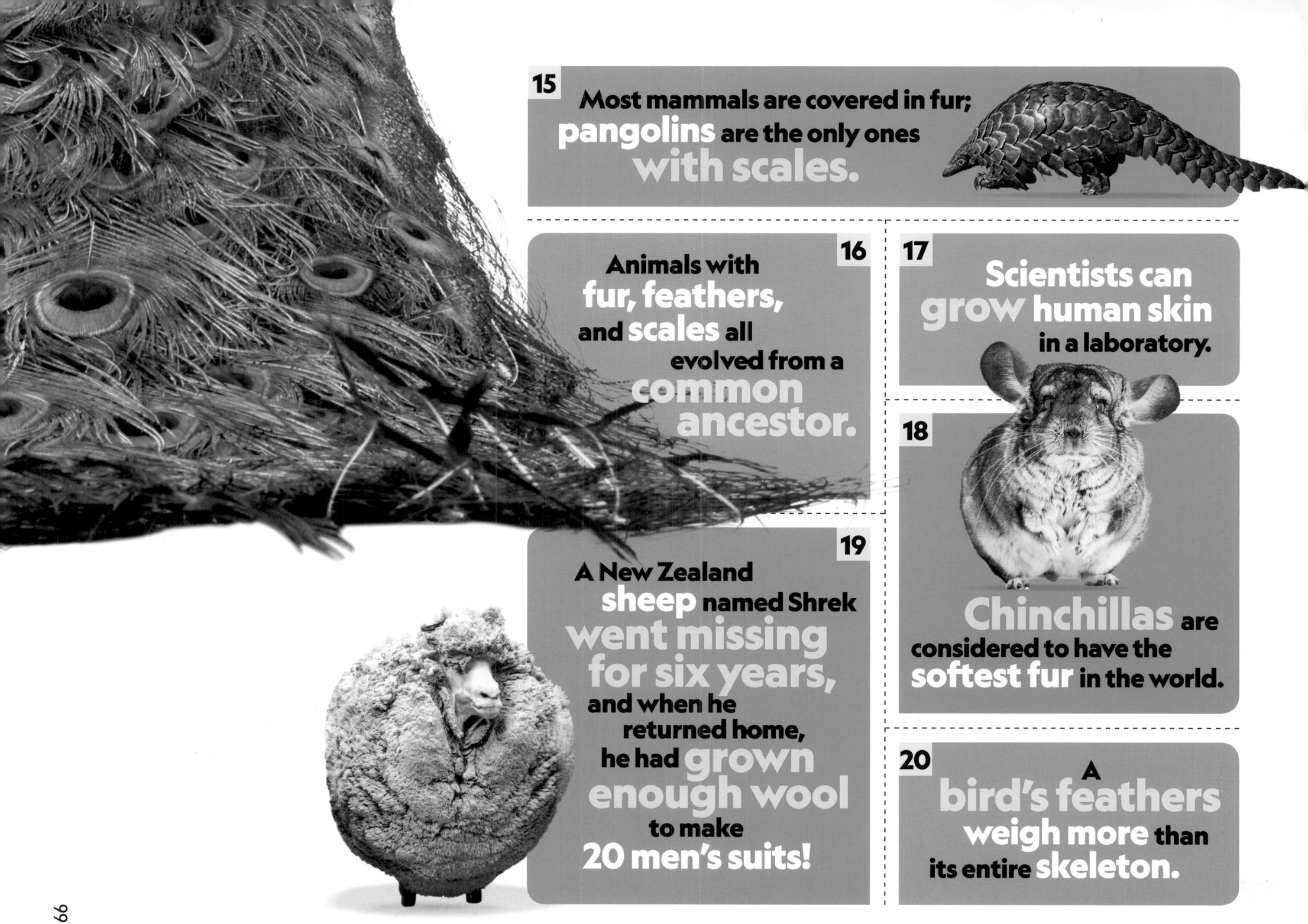

15 Most mammals are covered in fur; **pangolins** are the only ones **with scales.**

16 Animals with **fur, feathers,** and **scales** all evolved from a **common ancestor.**

17 Scientists can **grow** human skin in a laboratory.

18 **Chinchillas** are considered to have the **softest fur** in the world.

19 A New Zealand **sheep** named Shrek **went missing for six years,** and when he returned home, he had **grown enough wool** to make **20 men's suits!**

20 A **bird's feathers weigh more** than its entire **skeleton.**

Wild Facts About Places That Thrill

1

The Formula Rossa in Abu Dhabi, United Arab Emirates, is the world's fastest roller coaster, speeding to 149 miles an hour (240 km/h) in under five seconds.

2

Tropical Islands Resort, Germany, is the world's largest indoor water park, with speedy waterslides plus the world's largest indoor rainforest.

3

At a theme park in Nantes, France, you can ride on a 40-foot (12-m)-tall mechanical elephant that walks through the park.

4

The original map that Walt Disney created for Disneyland sold for $708,000.

5

At Crocosaurus Cove in Australia, you can swim in a clear tube next to a 16-foot (4.9-m)-long saltwater crocodile.

6

One water park in the Bahamas has a 60-foot (18-m) waterslide that shoots riders through a see-through tunnel with dozens of real sharks swimming around it!

7

Aqualud park in France is home to a waterslide called the Black Hole, in which you ride through complete darkness.

8

IMG Worlds of Adventure in Dubai, United Arab Emirates, is the world's largest indoor amusement park, spanning 1.5 million square feet (139,355 sq m).

9

The Insanity is a ride that dangles you above Las Vegas, Nevada, U.S.A., spinning at 40 miles an hour (64 km/h).

10

Holiday World & Splashin' Safari in Indiana, U.S.A., is home to the world's longest water coaster, measuring at 1,763 feet (537 m), which is over three times longer than the Washington Monument is tall!

Alarming Facts About Deadly Animals

1

The geographic cone snail **shoots venom** from a **harpoon-like** structure on the **end of its nose.**

2

Travelers are banned from **Snake Island** in Brazil because it's **home to** golden lancehead vipers, whose venom can **melt human flesh.**

3

Some hunters in the rainforest use **poison dart frog toxins** on their **blow darts.**

4

The bombardier beetle can **shoot hot poison from its rear end** 500 times a second.

5

The wood tiger moth is the **first species known** to secrete **nasty fluids** from a specific body part depending on the predator—from the **abdomen for ants,** from the **neck for birds.**

6

The **tentacles** of the Portuguese man-of-war can be **up to 165 feet** (50 m) long.

7

The male **great bustard** bird impresses females by eating **blister beetles,** which contain a **poison** that rids the bird of parasites, helping it **look more attractive.**

8

The zombie worm **secretes acid** that is strong enough to **break down animal bone.**

9

The blue-ringed **octopus** is the **size of a golf ball** but carries venom **1,000 times** more powerful than **cyanide.**

10

The mouth of a wild **Komodo dragon** contains **powerful venom.** It will often bite its prey, tracking it until it **collapses.**

Music

Facts to Get Stuck in Your Head

1

The world's **smallest guitar** is only about **the size** of a human **blood cell.**

2

Big Carl—the nickname for the **world's largest tuba**—is **eight feet** (2.4 m) tall and needs **three people** to play it properly.

3

Talking drums were used in Africa for centuries to **send messages** over **long distances.**

4

The world record for **longest drum roll** is **12 hours,** 5 minutes, and 7 seconds.

5

The **first saxophone** was **made of wood,** not brass.

6

Many musical instruments have made their way into space, including a keyboard, a guitar, and a didgeridoo (a wind instrument native to Australia).

7

One of the first typewriters was called a "literary piano."

8

Zookeepers at the Smithsonian National Zoo in Washington, D.C., gave one of their elephants instruments such as harmonicas and a horn to play, using her trunk.

9

The Vegetable Orchestra performs around the world on instruments made of fresh vegetables, like a pumpkin drum, carrot flutes, and a celery guitar.

10

A man from Germany set a world record for cycling backward while playing a violin: 37.6 miles (60.45 km) in 5 hours and 8 seconds.

Extreme Weirdness

GORILLA FOOLS HUMANS

WHAT Ape robot

WHERE Bristol, England

DETAILS Call it Planet of the Fake Apes. The Bristol Zoo Gardens' "Wow! Gorillas" exhibit featured an animatronic ape and several five-foot (1.5-m)-tall fiberglass gorilla sculptures. The sculptures were later painted and decorated by local artists. What's next—papier-mâché penguins?

PIG ON WHEELS

WHAT Pig-shaped race car

WHERE Medellín, Colombia

DETAILS Oink, oink—er, honk, honk! Better get out of the way of this racing pig. The homemade car was one of many wacky vehicles that took part in a car festival. Wonder what other fun farm animals this swine swooped past?

BOATS GO SKIING

WHAT Snow kayaking

WHERE Otepää, Estonia

DETAILS Why sail on water when you can grab your boat and hit the slopes? Athletes at a ski resort raced in kayaks down a custom-made track of snow. Steering with their paddles, the racers glided over multiple snowbanks before finally crossing the finish line into a pool of water. Snow's up, dude!

CHOCOLATE DRESS

WHAT Candy clothing

WHERE Edinburgh, Scotland

DETAILS How do you celebrate National Chocolate Week? By wearing an entire outfit made of the sweet stuff. A Scottish designer created this chocolate look for a fashion show celebrating the tasty treat. In addition to the 110-pound (50-kg) dress, the model wore a chocolate hat and fan. That's one sweet-looking getup.

PIZZA BED

WHAT Pizza slice sleeping bag

WHERE Glen Mills, Pennsylvania, U.S.A.

DETAILS Do you dream about pizza? Well, now you can sleep in it! This cozy sleeping bag looks like a slice of pizza and comes with a choice of toppings that can be detached and used as cushions. Among the comfy add-ons are broccoli, olives, pepperoni, and mushrooms. Hold the sauce, please.

T. REX SCORES GOAL

WHAT Dinosaur disguise

WHERE Carson, California, U.S.A.

DETAILS Who knew dinosaurs loved sports? A person in a *T. rex* costume kicked around a soccer ball during a game between California's LA Galaxy and Washington's Seattle Sounders. The fake predator hit the field to promote a local museum. Sounds like a roaring good time!

1

To figure out the **outside temperature** (in degrees Fahrenheit) add 40 to **the number** of **chirps** a cricket **makes** in 14 seconds.

2

When **humans are cold,** our bodies start to **shiver** to help raise our **body temperature.**

3

You are made up of **70 percent water.** When your body loses **just one percent** you'll start to **feel thirsty.**

4

Your body **loses heat** 25 times **faster in water** than it does in the **outside air.**

5

From 1914 to 1916, explorer **Ernest Shackleton** and his crew **survived** after being **stranded in the Antarctic.**

Facts About Survival to Keep You Going

6

The diving bell spider can **live underwater** by creating a **bubble-like** web around itself—it needs to come up for air only **once a day!**

7

Tardigrades **can survive** for more than **100 years without water.**

8

A former park ranger in Virginia, U.S.A., holds the record for **surviving the most lightning strikes—7!**

9

Karakul, a type of **sheep, store extra fat in their tails** so they can **survive** harsh conditions.

10

You can **start a campfire** using **an orange.**

Stinky Facts to Sniff Out

1

A **skunk's spray** can cause nearby **predators** to **choke** and become **temporarily blind.**

2

The eastern **skunk cabbage** gives off a skunk-like smell to **attract flies** to pollinate it.

3

When an Africanized honeybee feels **threatened,** it **alerts its fellow bees** by releasing a scent that smells **like banana.**

4

The sea hare **sea slug** releases a **smelly, slimy, purple ink** that makes the slug **taste worse** to predators.

Scientists say that **crested auklet** birds **smell like tangerines!**

6

5

A **vanilla-scented goo** that comes from a **beaver's behind** is sometimes used as a natural **food flavoring.**

Gingko tree seeds release a strong **vomit-like** smell to **attract animals** to eat them and **spread** the seeds.

8

7

Humans are considered one of the **smelliest mammals** because they release odors from nearly **every part** of their **bodies.**

9

The **citronella ant** emits a **lemony odor** to defend itself.

10

Hyenas

produce a scent from their rear ends that they use to **communicate** with one another.

Weird Facts About Wild Animals

1

The babirusa is known as a **"pig-deer"**—it needs to **grind down** its tusks, otherwise they will grow back **into its skull.**

2

The white yeti crab is covered in a fluffy **furlike coat** that **helps the crab** find food in the deep sea.

3

When the southern right whale **swims,** it constantly **leaps out** of **the water.**

4

With a tiny head and a **long neck** for reaching branches, the gerenuk antelope is known as the **"giraffe gazelle"!**

5

Snub-nosed monkeys have an **upturned nose** that tends to **collect water**—the primates often **sneeze** to clear their **"nose puddles."**

6

The **dementor wasp,** named after creatures from the **Harry Potter** series, **injects venom** into cockroaches that makes them slow and **zombie-like.**

7

The tanuki, or "raccoon dog," looks like a **fluffy raccoon** but is more closely **related to a wolf.**

8

The flattie spider **doesn't make a web** and instead **spins around** on one of its eight legs to **snatch its prey.**

9

The Sunda **flying lemur isn't actually a lemur** and it **can't fly.** However, it can cover more than 328 feet (100 m) **in a single glide!**

10

The **tusk of a narwhal** is **actually a tooth** that can grow up to approximately **nine feet** (2.7 m) long.

Birthday Facts That Take the Cake

1

The record for the **most expensive** birthday cake = **$75 million!**

2

One of the three songs **sung most often** in the English language is **"Happy Birthday to You."**

3

The Smithsonian National Zoo celebrated a young **panda's birthday** with a **frozen "cake"** made mostly of juices, fruits, and veggies.

4

In Italy, people **tug on the earlobes** of the lucky birthday boy or girl to **wish them good luck.**

5

Instead of celebrating **individual birthdays,** people from Vietnam typically celebrate **all birthdays** on **New Year's Day.**

6

Piñatas in Mexico are often **filled with fruit,** not just candy.

7

It's tradition in Jamaica to **throw flour** at the birthday boy or girl, sometimes **soaking** the person with water first so the flour **sticks better!**

8

Instead of a traditional birthday cake, **Danish** children receive a **"cakeman,"** and the birthday child **takes the head.**

Turn the page for more fantastic birthday facts!

9

The record for **the most lit candles** on a cake at one time was **72,585.**

10

Eating a plate of **long noodles** is a **Chinese birthday tradition** that symbolizes living a **long life.**

11

Sprinkles are called **"hundreds and thousands"** in Australia.

12

The melody of "Happy Birthday to You" was **written in 1893** by **two sisters** from Kentucky, U.S.A.

13

In New Zealand, people **skip cakes** altogether and instead enjoy **sprinkles on top of toast,** called **"fairy bread."**

14

In the 1800s, during the Victorian era, **parents** used their **children's birthday parties** to **teach them manners.**

15

11 = The record for the **number of candles lit** by **someone's feet** in one minute!

16

It's **tradition** in some Canadian provinces to **smear butter** on the birthday boy or girl's **nose.**

17

The term **"birthday cake"** was **first used** in **1785.**

18

November 26 is **National Cake Day** in the United States.

19

In the U.S., the third Monday of February—**Presidents' Day**—was originally called Washington's Birthday in honor of **George Washington.**

20

In Russia, **birthday wishes** are usually carved into a **fruit pie crust.**

Fast Facts About Wild Rides

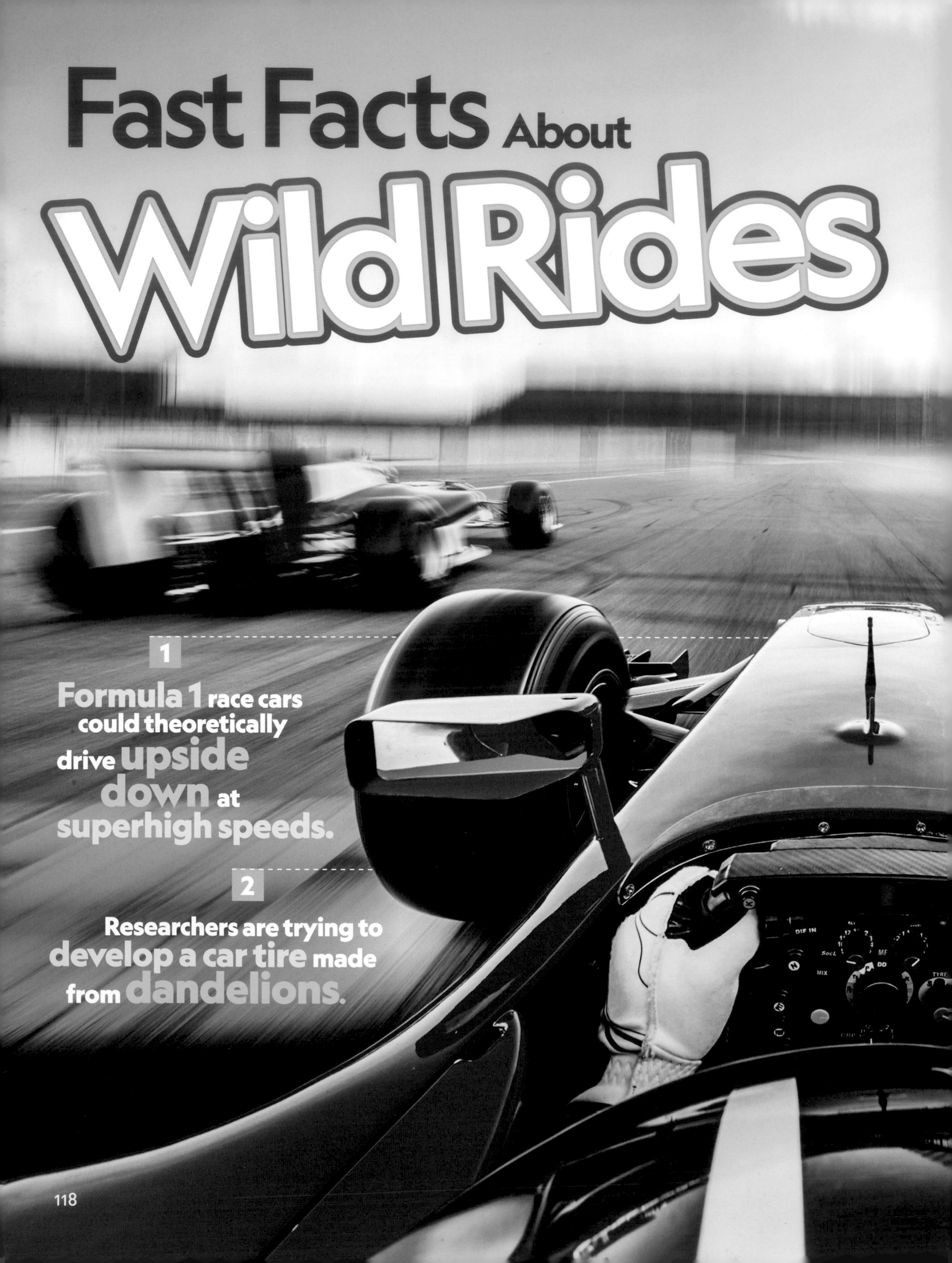

1

Formula 1 race cars could theoretically drive upside down at superhigh speeds.

2

Researchers are trying to develop a car tire made from dandelions.

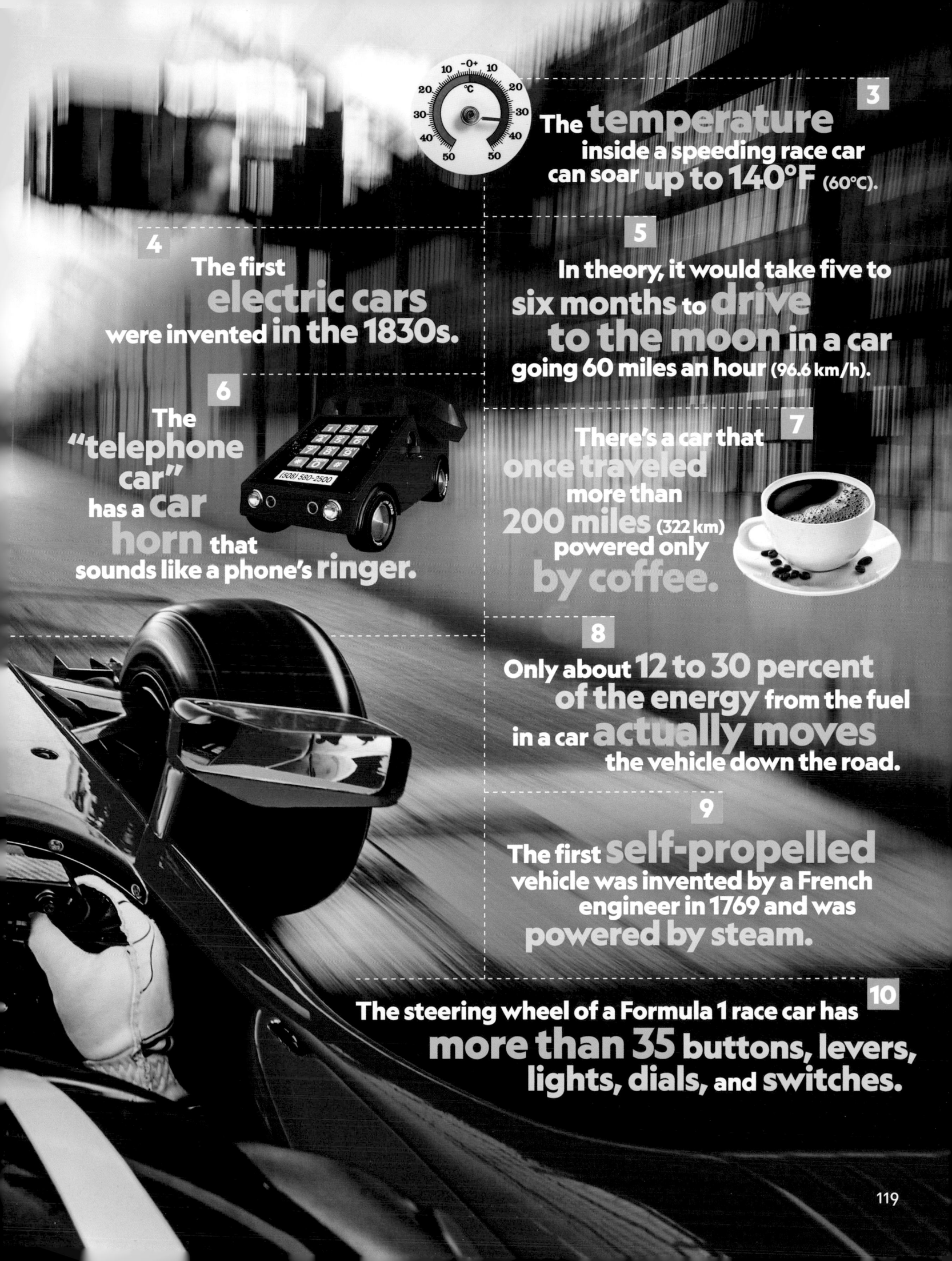

3

The **temperature** inside a speeding race car can soar **up to 140°F** (60°C).

4

The first **electric cars** were invented in the 1830s.

5

In theory, it would take five to **six months** to **drive to the moon** in a car going 60 miles an hour (96.6 km/h).

6

The **"telephone car"** has a **car horn** that sounds like a phone's **ringer.**

7

There's a car that **once traveled** more than **200 miles** (322 km) powered only **by coffee.**

8

Only about **12 to 30 percent of the energy** from the fuel in a car **actually moves** the vehicle down the road.

9

The first **self-propelled** vehicle was invented by a French engineer in 1769 and was **powered by steam.**

10

The steering wheel of a Formula 1 race car has **more than 35** buttons, levers, lights, dials, and switches.

Funky Facts About Fruits and Veggies

1

Bananas are considered **berries.**

2

The city of Chicago, Illinois, U.S.A., was named after the Native American word *chicagoua*, for a type of **garlic plant.**

3

Cathead, Winter Banana, and Captain Kidd are all names of **apples!**

4

At the local Watermelon Thump Festival in Luling, Texas, U.S.A., locals compete in a **seed-spitting contest.**

5

Lettuce and **leafy greens** were the first foods **grown in space.**

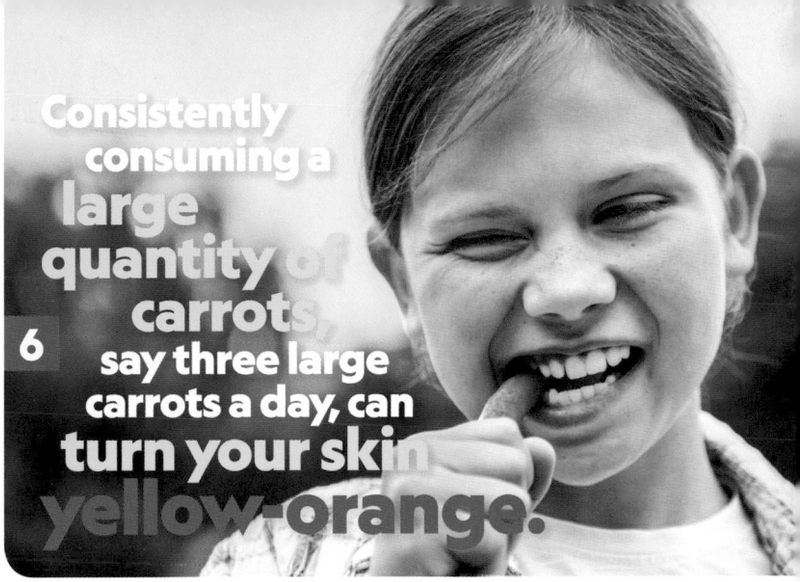

6

Consistently consuming a **large quantity of carrots,** say three large carrots a day, can **turn your skin yellow-orange.**

7

Chili peppers are actually **fruits.**

8

The black sapote fruit looks like an **overripe green tomato** on the outside, but looks and **tastes like chocolate pudding** on the inside.

9

The original **nickname for eggplant** in Europe was **"crazy apple."**

10

The **durian fruit,** found in Asia, is so **notoriously stinky** that it's **banned** from Singapore's trains.

1

Some say you can still **hear the banjo** twangs of a **former prisoner** at the famous **Alcatraz prison** in California, U.S.A.

2

People have claimed to see a **floating vampire** at **Highgate Cemetery** in England.

3

Former U.S. president William Howard Taft was reportedly **haunted** by the ghost of a **15-year-old** boy in the **White House.**

4

You can go on a tour to visit an **underground ghost town** called Mary King's Close that is said to be one of **Scotland's most haunted** places.

5

At the Stanley Hotel in Colorado, U.S.A., you might hear the **ghosts of children laughing** or the ghost of Mrs. Stanley **playing the piano.**

6

In York, England, a ghost named **Mad Alice laughs** as people walk by, and the ghost of **the Grey Lady** will **tickle the necks** of tourists at the Georgian Theatre Royal.

7

Poveglia Island, Italy, is considered to be **so haunted** that the government **no longer** allows **access to the public.**

8

At an **old fort** in New York, U.S.A., legend says a **headless soldier** has been seen emerging **from a well** at midnight.

9 If you want to **take a photo** of Robert, a supposedly **haunted doll** on display at a Florida, U.S.A. museum, you need to politely **ask his permission.** If he **tilts his head,** that means yes!

10 A cemetery on the island of Barbados claims that **its coffins** have mysteriously **moved by themselves.**

Spooky Facts About Haunted Places

1

People can **celebrate all things garlic** at the annual garlic festival in California, U.S.A., including **garlic ice cream.**

2

Proud Corgi owners bring hundreds of corgis to **Corgi Beach Day** in California where the dogs can **frolic** among thousands of bacon- and **chicken-flavored bubbles!**

3

Chase a **nine-pound** (4-kg) **wheel of cheese down a hill** in the U.K. at the annual Cheese-Rolling event.

4

In honor of a savory food called Yorkshire pudding, people **race down rivers** in **boats made of flour, egg, and water** in the U.K.

5

The **Bun Scrambling** Competition in Hong Kong invites competitors to **climb a tall tower** covered **in buns** and collect as many as they can in three minutes!

Facts About Fun Festivals to Celebrate

6

The **Night of the Radishes** = An annual event in which people compete by **carving intricate shapes into radishes.**

7

The three-day **Battle of the Oranges** takes place annually in Italy when teams **adorned in armor** storm the street **hurling oranges** at each other.

8

Coffin Races = 70 teams dress in **spooky costumes,** racing coffins down the **main avenue** of Manitou Springs, Colorado, U.S.A.

9

Every year, about **22,000 people** join the world's largest **tomato fight** in Spain.

10

If you aren't competing in the **Air Guitar World Championships,** you can still attend and take **air guitar workshops** with air guitar champions.

Puzzling Facts About Unsolved Mysteries

1

According to local legend, a **boy and a girl** with **green skin** arrived in Woolpit, England, in the 12th century and claimed to come from **another world.**

2

Taos Hum is a **strange buzzing noise** in the town of Taos, New Mexico, U.S.A.—**no one knows** where the sound is **coming from.**

3

A scientist once received a **72-second signal** from the constellation Sagittarius, and **who or what** the signal came from is **still unclear.**

4

In 1947, a **balloon crashed** at a ranch in Roswell, New Mexico, but many believe it was **actually a UFO** that the government tried to **cover up.**

5

In 1912, a man named Wilfrid Voynich purchased a **mysterious medieval book** that was written in a **language** and alphabet that **no one can translate.**

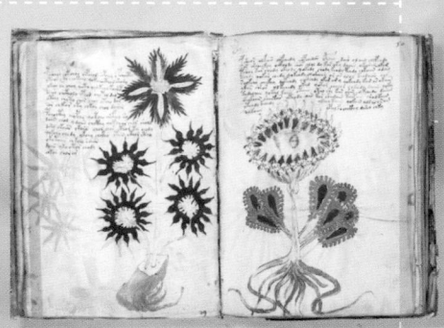

6

A farmer once claimed to have seen a **whole Bigfoot family** running through his ranch **carrying a pig.**

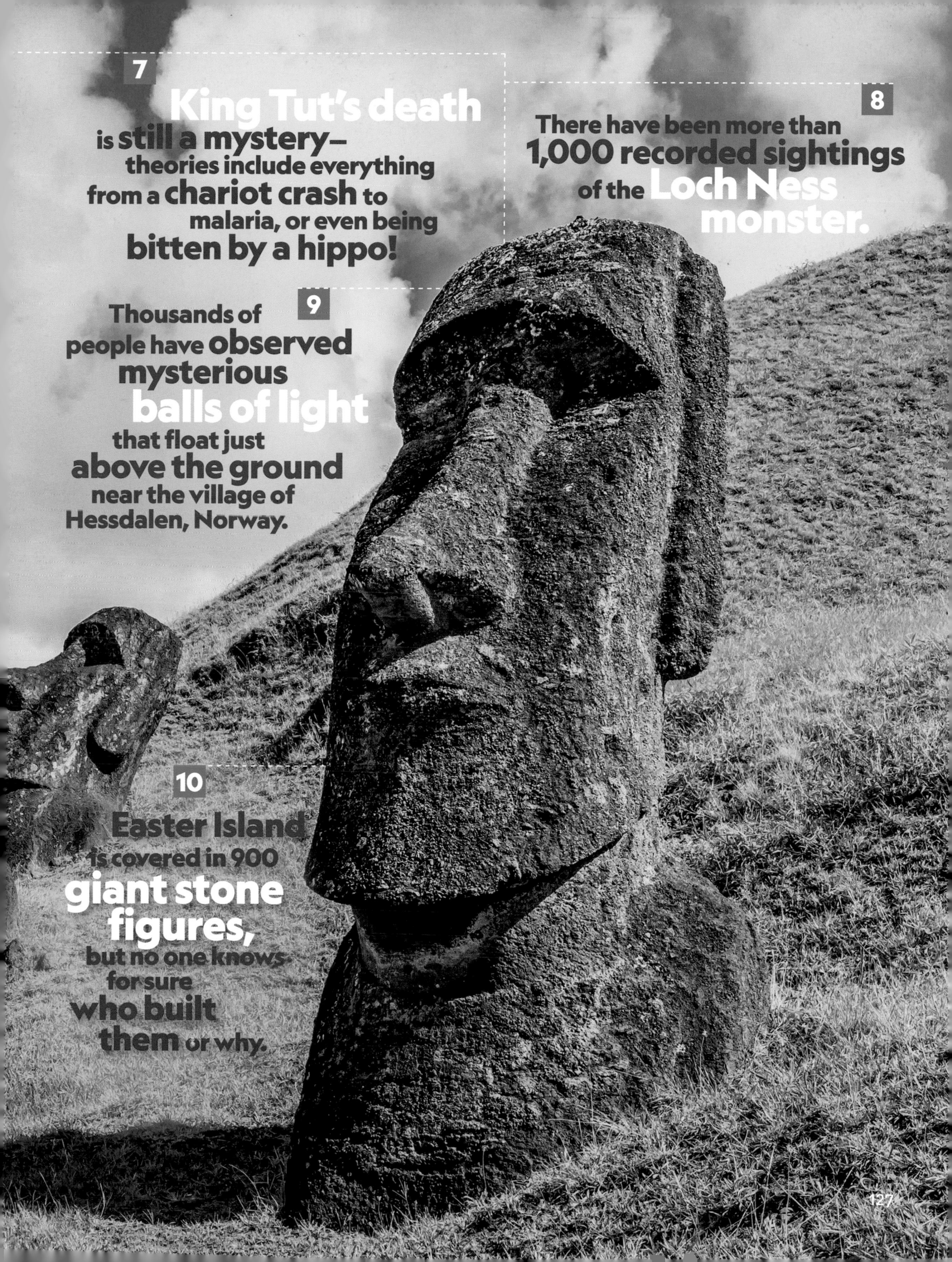

7

King Tut's death is still a mystery– theories include everything from a chariot crash to malaria, or even being bitten by a hippo!

8

There have been more than 1,000 recorded sightings of the Loch Ness monster.

9

Thousands of people have observed mysterious balls of light that float just above the ground near the village of Hessdalen, Norway.

10

Easter Island is covered in 900 giant stone figures, but no one knows for sure who built them or why.

KANGAROO VS. WALLABY

Kangaroos and wallabies are both marsupials, carrying their adorable young in their comfy, cozy pouches. But there are some major characteristics that set these two hind-legged hoppers apart. The most distinct difference is their size! Wallabies have much shorter hind legs, and they grow to be anywhere from roughly one to two feet (30 cm to 61 cm) tall, whereas kangaroos are much larger, sizing up to a height between three and eight feet (1 to 2.4 m) tall. Their size has a great deal to do with the different habitats they live in—kangaroos have longer legs to help them move quickly through open terrain; wallabies have shorter legs to help them be more agile in more wooded areas. These habitats also inspire their eating habits—kangaroos eat mostly grass, whereas wallabies munch on a variety of both grasses and plants.

What's the Difference?

Check out these similar pairings and see how you can determine this from that!

WEATHER VS. CLIMATE

What's the difference between weather and climate? Time! Weather generally refers to shorter periods of certain conditions. It might be sunny or raining—even changing one minute to the next—or we might be anxiously watching the news to see if schools will have a snow day! On the other hand, climate refers to the patterns that affect a particular area over a long period of time, given the average weather a specific region might see. For instance, Florida, U.S.A., is more prone to consistent, hot, humid weather and hurricanes, whereas Colorado, U.S.A., is more prone to dry weather, different seasons, and wildfires.

BANANA VS. PLANTAIN

These slender, delicious fruits both change colors, as well as flavor, at different stages of ripeness, but why would someone choose to eat a banana over a plantain or vice versa? Plantains are often cooked before they are eaten because eating one raw can be tough. They have less sugar and are a little starchier than bananas, giving them a more savory, dry texture. Because of this, they are often paired with other savory foods, like onions, whereas bananas tend to be paired with sweeter foods like yogurt or cereal, or set aflame in brown sugar for bananas foster. Bananas are much moister, making them easier to eat without being cooked.

ENVY VS. JEALOUSY

These two words have confounded the laws of language since the 13th century! Depending on who you ask, there isn't much of a difference and they are often used interchangeably, but there are a few instances when it might be better to choose one word over the other. "Envy" tends to be used more often when someone lacks something that someone else has, whether looks, prized possessions, or even a certain stature in life. "Jealousy," on the other hand, usually refers to an emotion someone feels when something he or she already possesses is threatened; jealousy often comes into play in friendships and relationships.

RACQUETBALL VS. SQUASH

Both involve hitting a ball fast and wild in a fairly small enclosed room using some kind of racquet (racquetball) or racket (squash), but that might be as far as it goes for similarities when it comes to these two swatting sports! Racquetball started in America; squash began much earlier in England. In squash, the racket and ball are smaller than those in racquetball. But in racquetball the ball is much lighter, giving it a higher bounce and making for a fast-paced game, especially when there are practically no boundary lines and any surface can be used to bounce the ball off of, including the ceiling! In comparison, squash does have boundary lines, so no ceiling bouncing allowed. Thank goodness it does have boundaries, because with a heavier ball there is less bounce time, meaning a player needs to get to the ball quickly before it bounces again!

CRICKET VS. GRASSHOPPER

These leaping, singing creatures are full of small and big differences that aren't always clear unless you're paying close attention. Crickets and grasshoppers both have antennae, but the cricket's are long, while the grasshopper's are short. But don't mistake their antennae for "ears," as they don't help them hear! A grasshopper's "ears" are in their abdomen, whereas crickets have them in their front legs. Both crickets and grasshoppers stridulate, which produces the cool music you hear coming from crickets that rub their wings together or grasshoppers when they rub their legs together. It's unlikely you'll hear their sweet tunes battling against one another, as grasshoppers usually play during the day and crickets at night.

Tricky Facts About Magicians

1

The Merlin Award is an award given to the **best magician** of the year from around the world.

2

Houdini's most famous trick was making an **elephant "disappear"** in a box by hiding it behind a mirror that reflected the empty space of the box, making the box appear empty.

3

Project Magic is a program that teaches people with disabilities how to **do magic tricks** to enhance motor skills and gain self-confidence.

4

The **Bullet Catch** is a magic trick in which a gun is fired at a magician who must "catch" the bullet with his or her mouth, hand, or other object.

5

Magician David Blaine trapped his **entire body in ice** for 63 hours, 42 minutes, and 15 seconds on a busy street in New York City.

6

Muhammad Ali wasn't just one of the greatest boxers of all time—he also did magic tricks.

7

Magicians sometimes **spend years** perfecting one magic trick.

8

Jasper Maskelyne was a magician who helped **fight the Nazis** in WWII by hiding tools and maps inside everyday objects like playing cards.

9

Magicians must take a magician's oath to **protect the secrets** of the trade before another magician teaches them their tricks.

10

Charles, **Prince of Wales,** is a member of the "Magic Circle," an exclusive club for magicians.

Extreme Facts About Adventures

1

A Zorb is a giant **plastic ball** that a human can get inside of to **roll down a hill, float on water,** or even **play football.**

2

More than **400 people** worldwide have climbed the **Seven Summits,** which involves reaching the **highest mountain peak** on each continent.

3

As a popular pastime in India, people have **combined the sports** of limbo and roller skating into **"limbo skating,"** which is sometimes done **under cars!**

4

Extreme ironing is when people **iron clothes** in **weird situations,** including ironing while **skydiving** and ironing while **kayaking** rapids.

5

The first person to **walk on a tightrope** over **Niagara Falls** walked 1,300 feet (396 m). He then went back across **performing stunts.**

6

An Italian man **set the record** for the **deepest cycling underwater** at 218 feet, 11 inches (66.5 m).

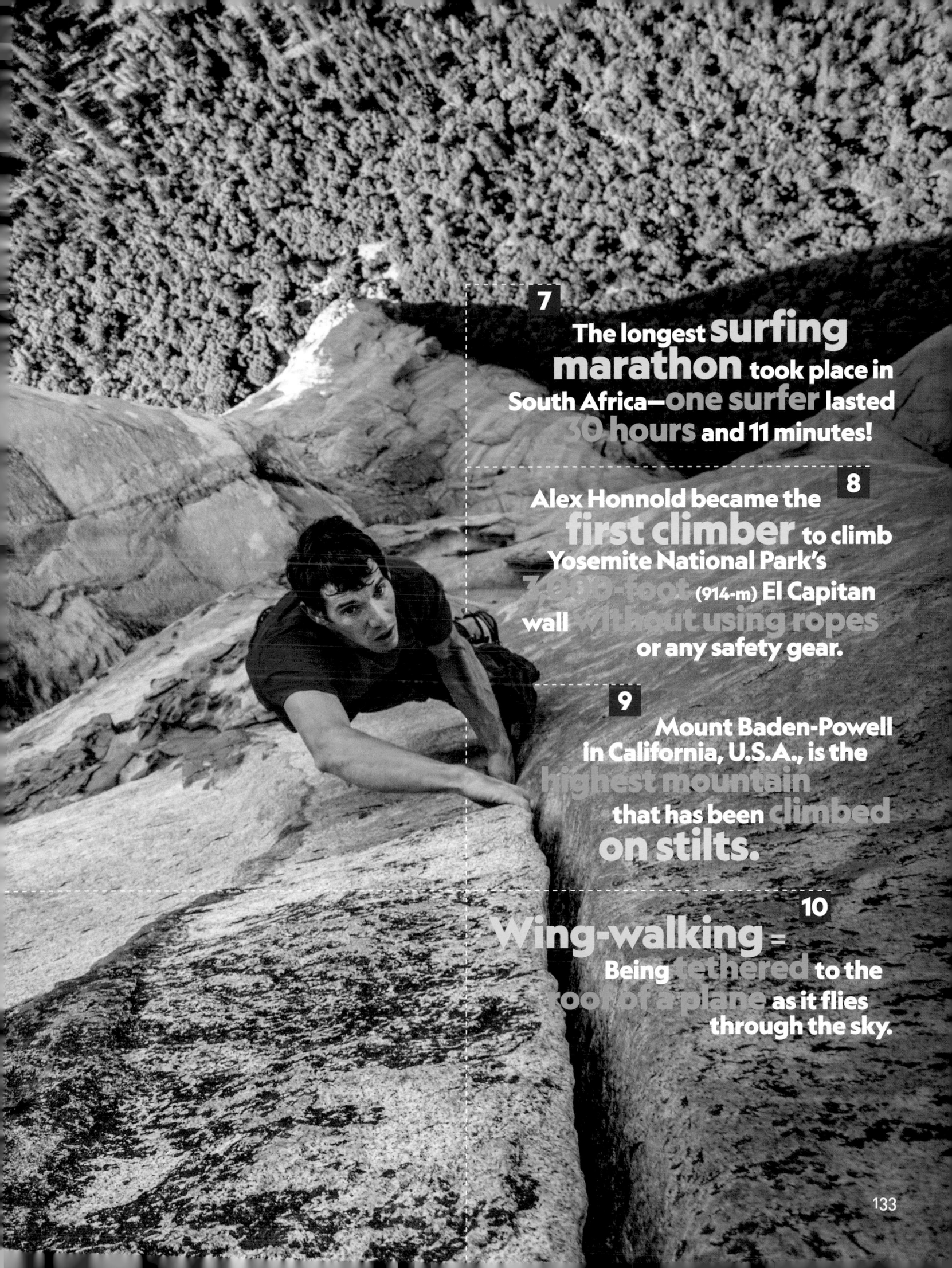

7

The longest **surfing marathon** took place in South Africa—**one surfer** lasted **30 hours** and 11 minutes!

8

Alex Honnold became the **first climber** to climb Yosemite National Park's **7,310-foot** (914-m) El Capitan wall **without using ropes** or any safety gear.

9

Mount Baden-Powell in California, U.S.A., is the **highest mountain** that has been **climbed on stilts.**

10

Wing-walking = Being **tethered** to the **roof of a plane** as it flies through the sky.

Shhh!... Secret Facts About Spies

1

Spies have used weapons disguised as lipstick and pipes!

2

In the 1960s, the CIA, the U.S. spy agency, provided travel disguise kits to spies.

3

A real-life spy known as "the limping lady" had a prosthetic leg that she hid documents in.

4

Secret maps used to help spies escape to safety were hidden in playing cards in which the top layer of the card could be peeled away after being soaked in water.

5

Spies sometimes passed messages by leaving them inside a dead rat covered in hot sauce on the street—the hot sauce helped scare away any animals that tried to eat it.

6

The CIA issued radio transmitters camouflaged as pieces of dog poop.

8

The first insect-size aerial vehicle created to spy on the enemy looked like a dragonfly.

7

Cameras used to be hidden in many items, like ties, shoes, walking sticks, pens, wallets, and handbags.

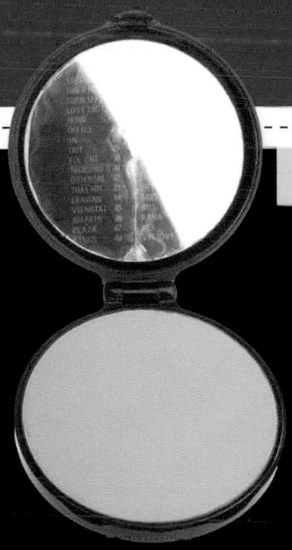

9

A modified makeup compact was used to help decipher codes in mirrors.

10

During WWI, cameras were strapped to pigeons to capture pictures of enemy weapons and to help create battle maps.

Glowing Facts About Jellyfish

1 There is evidence that jellyfish lived in the ancient world at least 400 million years before dinosaurs existed!

2 Some types of jellyfish will eat peanut butter.

Crown jelly

3 The **lion's mane** jellyfish can grow more than **100 feet** (30.5 m) **long** and up to seven feet (2 m) wide, rivaling the size of the **blue whale.**

4 Jellyfish are **made of** more than **95 percent water.**

5 Jellyfish **aren't fish—** they're actually **related to coral!**

6 Not only does the **gooey, soft body** of a jellyfish not contain **a single bone,** but it also **doesn't have a head,** a heart, a brain, eyes, ears, or a nose!

7 A jellyfish's **tentacles** can **still sting** even when they **break apart** from the **jellyfish's body.**

8 Scientists have been **extracting a protein** from jellyfish to **power nanobots** (teeny tiny robots)!

9 Many jellyfish are considered **"Medusa"** jellyfish, which refers to a monster from Greek mythology with **wild snakes** for hair.

10 One species of jellyfish is **nicknamed "pink meanie"** due to its **intense sting** and deep color.

Funny Facts to Keep You Giggling

1 The sound of your laugh changes depending on whether you're chuckling with pals or strangers.

2 Between 10 and 15 minutes of laughing burns between 10 and 40 calories.

3 Laughter reduces stress.

4 **Gelotology** = The **scientific study** of **laughter** and its effects on the body.

5 **Laughing** at a joke requires activity in **five different areas** of **the brain.**

6 **Apes and rats** appear to laugh **when tickled.**

7 Laughter can **strengthen friendships.**

8 There was an **outbreak** of **contagious laughter** in an African town that lasted for **several months** straight.

9 You're 30 times more **likely to laugh** when you're around **friends** than when **you're alone.**

10 Before humans used **spoken language,** some scientists believe they **used laughter** to **communicate** with each other.

1

The three-inch (8-cm) ruby-throated **hummingbird** can flap its wings up to **200 times** per second when **impressing a mate.**

2

Bumblebee bats weigh around **.07 ounce** (2 g)—that's only slightly more than an **index card!**

3

The Japanese **dwarf flying squirrel** hangs **upside down** on a branch while eating.

4

Because of their small stature, **mini horses** are used for a variety of **therapy** outlets, visiting more than **25,000 people** each year.

5

Pygmy hippos are **half as tall** as **regular hippos.**

6

A **tiny mite** the size of a sesame seed is the **fastest animal** on the planet.

7

Acmella nana is the world's **tiniest snail**, with a shiny, **see-through shell** that measures just .027 inch (.07 cm) tall.

8

The **pygmy marmoset** is the **smallest primate** in the world.

9

The record for the **smallest horse** is **17 inches** (43 cm) tall to the withers (shoulder blades).

10

Pygmy hedgehogs are **lactose intolerant**—no cheese, please!

Itty-Bitty Facts About Tiny Animals

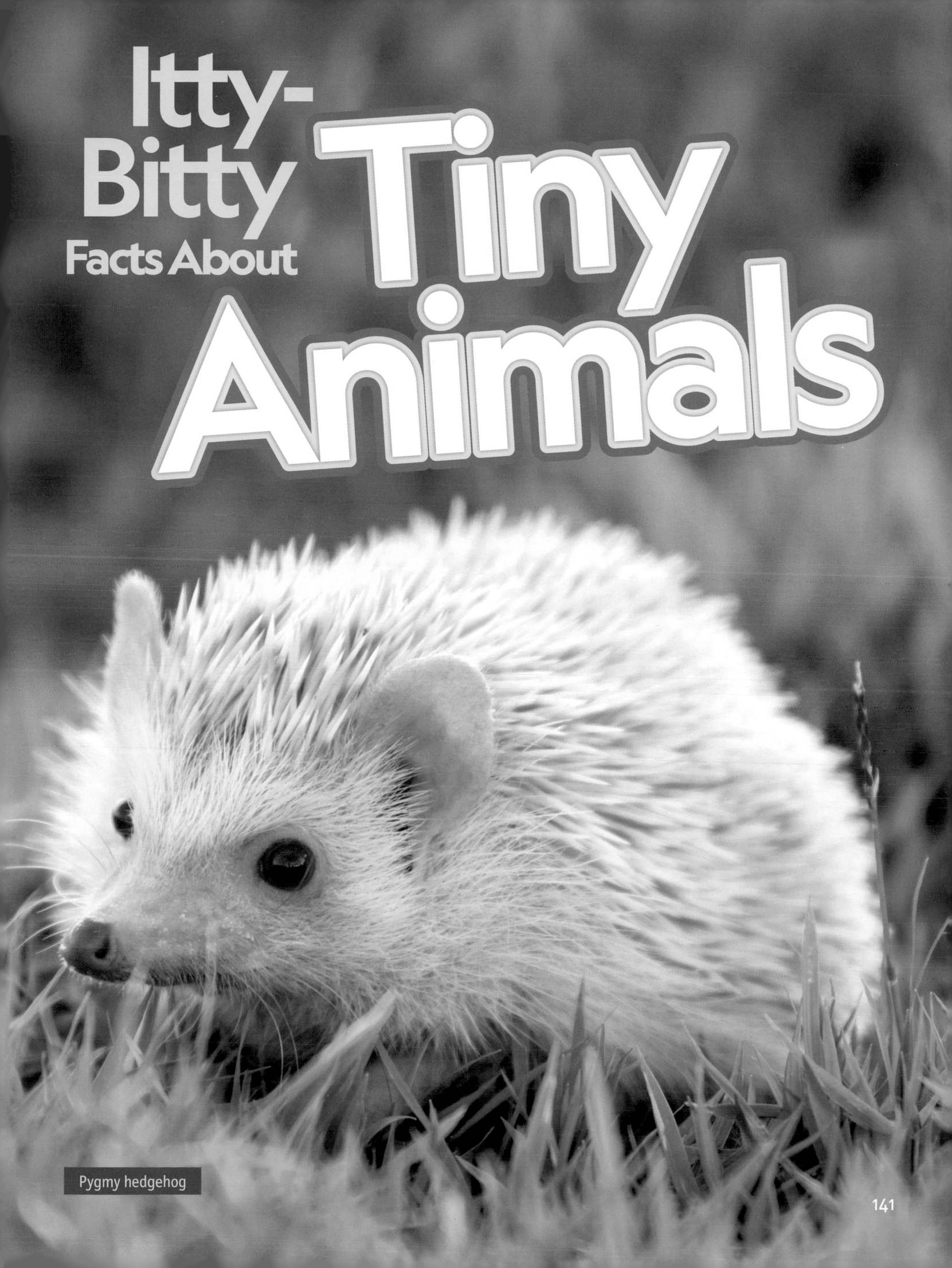

Pygmy hedgehog

A Gallery of Amusing Facts About Museums

1

The Museum of Bad Art has an entire section dedicated to paintings with blue people in them.

2

The Cancún Underwater Museum in Mexico has 500 life-size structures underwater that people can visit by glass-bottom boat, snorkeling, or scuba diving.

3

The Vent Haven Museum in Kentucky, U.S.A., houses hundreds of ventriloquist dummies.

4

The International Cryptozoology Museum in Maine, U.S.A., claims to have poop samples from Bigfoot.

5

The **Lunchbox Museum** in Georgia, U.S.A., has **more than 2,000** lunch boxes.

6

The Sulabh International **Museum of Toilets** in India traces the **4,500-year history** of the toilet, and it even has a toilet that **looks like a bookcase** on display.

The **Salt and Pepper** Shaker Museum in Tennessee, U.S.A., boasts **over 20,000** pairs of **shakers.**

8

7

There is a **lawn mower** museum in Great Britain where you can view **lawn mowers** of the **rich and famous.**

9

Head to the **Mütter Museum** in Philadelphia, Pennsylvania, U.S.A., to see a piece of **Albert Einstein's brain.**

10

The **Mustard Museum** in Wisconsin, U.S.A., has **5,992 jars** of mustard on display from 70 countries, plus a mustard **vending machine.**

Mountain Majesty Comes in Many Shades

Rainbow-colored foothills stretch for miles, their bright ridges popping against the blue sky. Boasting red, gold, orange, yellow, and blue stripes, the slopes look as if they belong in a sci-fi movie. But these formations are real, located right here on planet Earth. Part of Zhangye Danxia National Geopark in north-central China, the all-natural rock rainbows took millions of years—and a lot of shaking, rattling, and rolling—to form.

LASTING LAYERS

The hills of Zhangye Danxia (pronounced JANyeah DAN-siah) are nestled in a basin against the Qilian Mountains in China's Gansu Province. Covering about a hundred square miles (259 sq km), the slopes are hundreds of feet tall. Many have several stripes of color. How did these hills get their painted look? This landscape is made of layers of rock called strata. Similar to a tiered cake, it was created one layer at a time. The first sheet formed some 24 million years ago. Wind and water eroded parts of the land surrounding the basin, grinding it into sediment (or bits of rock). The pieces settled across the basin floor like a thick blanket, and eventually the sediment hardened. Over time, changes in climate affected the rate of erosion and appearance of the sediment that was produced from rocks surrounding the basin. Each new erosion phase brought a new color of sediment into the basin, in time creating another sheet of rock on top of the old one. This process happened over and over again until the basin was covered with hundreds of layers.

Danxia means "rosy cloud" in Chinese.

Red layers of rock come from iron that has rusted.

The continent crash that made these slopes also made the Himalaya!

CRUNCH TIME

The colorful formations in the basin at Gansu may have remained hidden under its top layer if not for a geological event that was literally shaking up the whole region. It all started in Earth's lithosphere. This is the outer layer of the planet, which is divided into huge plates that are constantly moving. Sometimes the movement of the plates slowly pushes up land on the surface and eventually creates hills and mountains.

SMASHING STRIPES

About 50 million years ago, the plate that carries the country we now call India began to collide with the plate that holds the rest of Asia. The crash was so powerful that it pushed chunks of land just south of the spot where Zhangye Danxia is located. Here, jagged mounds of earth rose over millions of years, revealing the ground's multicolored stripes. (The land was tilted as it was forced upward, which is why the layers run diagonally rather than horizontally.) Weathering and erosion smoothed over the rugged rocks and formed the rounded hills that you can see now.

A COLORFUL DRAW

In 2011, the Chinese government declared Zhangye Danxia a national park. Thousands of people visit every year to check out one of nature's ultimate art projects. But the rocky spot isn't done changing. Natural forces such as erosion continue to slowly transform the landscape. So, in another 24 million years, the area may look totally different. You'll just need a time machine to actually see those changes!

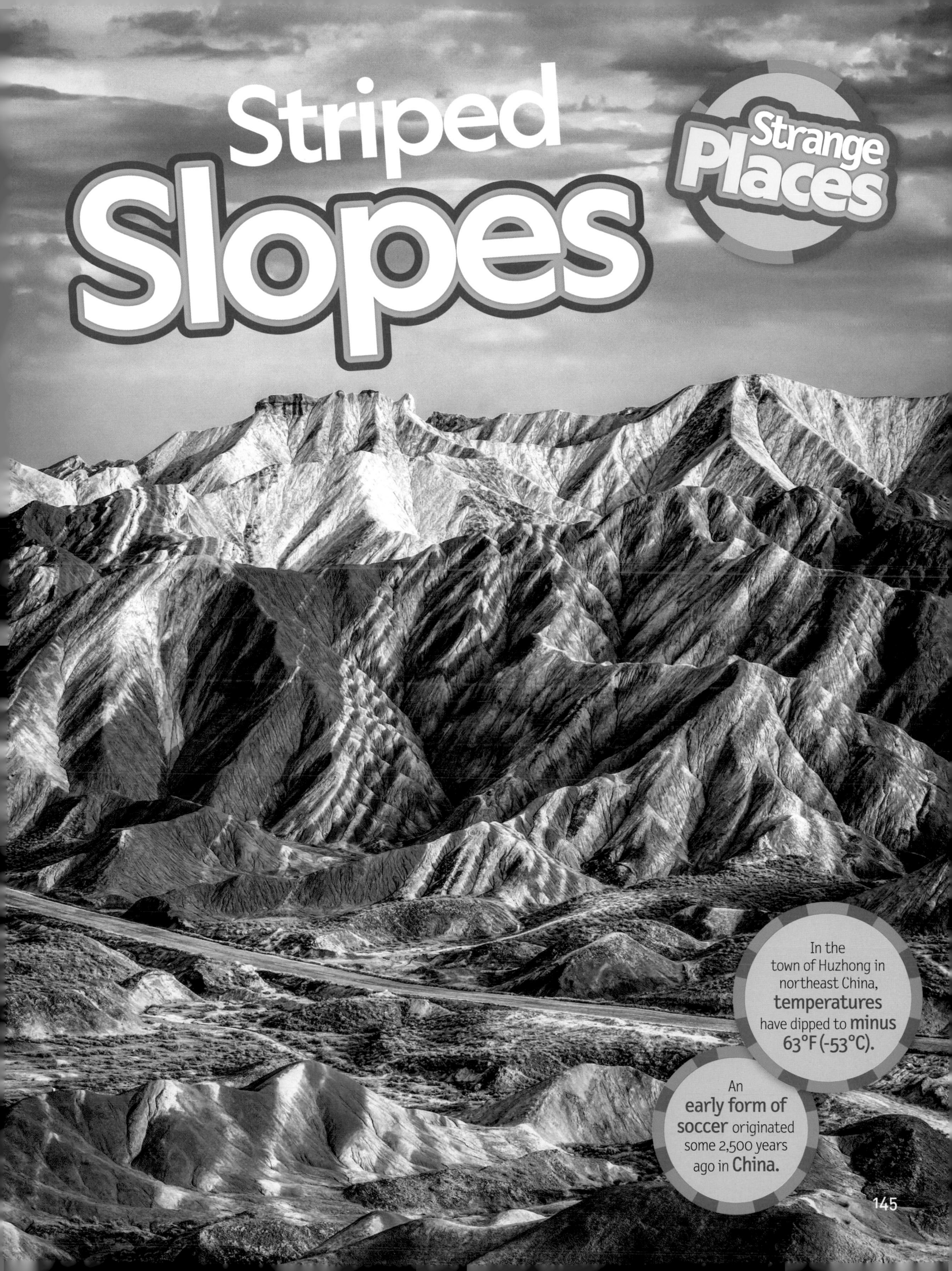

Striped Slopes

Strange Places

In the town of Huzhong in northeast China, **temperatures** have dipped to **minus 63°F (-53°C).**

An **early form of soccer** originated some 2,500 years ago in **China.**

Bright Facts About Biolumi

1 The bobtail squid has a specialized **light organ** that makes it seem **invisible** while it hunts.

2 The **U.S. Navy** monitors bioluminescence because some types of **algae** have been known to **endanger** military missions.

3 The **anglerfish** uses bioluminescence to **attract its prey.**

4 Bioluminescent Bay in Mosquito Bay, Puerto Rico, holds a **world record** for the **brightest** bioluminescent bay.

5 In Toyama Bay, Japan, the firefly squid creates **flashes of bright blue** that **people can see** between March and June.

Jervis Bay, Australia

nescence

6

The cookiecutter shark has a small **glowing patch** on its underbelly **in the shape** of a **small fish** to lure prey.

7

When the Atolla jellyfish is **attacked**, it sets off a **light display** called the **"burglar alarm"** that can be seen up to **300 feet** (91 m) **away!**

8

Most **deep-sea** bioluminescent creatures create **blue** or **green** light.

9

For two weeks every May, a **swarm of fireflies** gather in the U.S.A.'s Great Smoky Mountains, putting on a **"fireworks show."**

10

In the Waitomo Caves in New Zealand, the walls **twinkle** with thousands of bioluminescent **glowworms.**

1
Mzee, a 130-year-old tortoise in Kenya, Africa, looked after Owen, a baby hippo rescued after he was washed out to sea by a tsunami.
2
Alpaca moms hum to comfort their babies.
3
A newborn red kangaroo is 100,000 times smaller than its mother.
4
A baby fish is called a fry.
5
A newly hatched alligator rides on its mother's head or in her mouth.
6
A baby sloth hangs from its mother's fur until it's about a year old.
7
Baby squirrels are called kits or kittens.

Adorable Facts About Baby Animals

8

Baby birds learn their mother's song before they hatch.

9

Blue whale calves can gain up to 200 pounds (91 kg) a day in their first year.

10

Hedgehogs are born with soft spikes that take about three weeks to harden.

Fun Facts to Bear in Mind

1

Sloth bears can close their nostrils so that their mouth has more power to suck bees out of the hive, like a vacuum.

2

U.S. president Theodore Roosevelt had a pet bear while in office.

3

Polar bears have black skin under their fur.

4

Most bears do not poop or pee while they hibernate.

Kermode bear

5

The **kermode bear,** often called a **"spirit bear,"** is a rare species of a **black bear** that has **white fur.**

6

License plates are shaped like **polar bears** in Canada's Northwest Territories.

7

A **mysterious chef** in San Diego, California, U.S.A., wears a **bear costume while he cooks** and hosts dinner parties in secret locations three times a week.

8

A bear helped **carry supplies** for the **Polish Army** in **World War II.**

9

All polar bears can trace their ancestry back to **one female brown bear** that lived over **20,000 years ago** in Ireland.

10

Sloth, sun, and **spectacled** bears **do not hibernate.**

Facts About Super Splurges

1

In 2005, the original HOLLYWOOD sign sold for $450,400.

2

A robot from a 1956 movie sold for $5.3 million, making it the most expensive movie prop ever sold!

3

A bed shaped like Cinderella's pumpkin-turned-coach starts at $47,500.

4

For $2 million, you can buy a sports car that can drive underwater.

5

Diamonds are a dog's best friend—you can buy a $3.2-million **dog collar** embedded with 1,600 diamonds.

6

A **grilled cheese** sandwich once sold for $28,000 online.

7

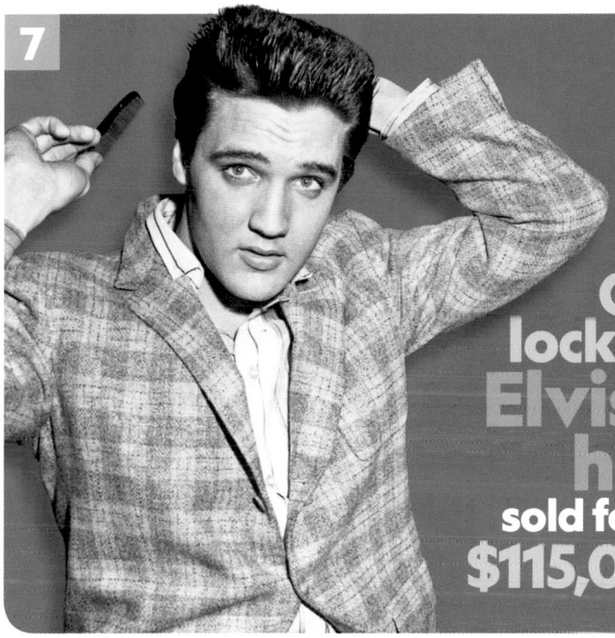

One lock of Elvis's hair sold for $115,000.

8

You can buy a **gold-encrusted donut** for $100.

9

A $1,770 **hamburger** at a London, England, restaurant included caviar sprinkled with gold leaf.

10

For nearly $7,000, you can buy a

dog bathtub

encrusted with more than 45,000 pink crystals.

Action-Packed Facts About Sports

1 In Japan, **snowball fighting,** called *yukigassen,* is an **official sport.**

2 Pato, the **national sport** of Argentina, is a mix of **polo and basketball.**

3 Some daredevils **cruise down active volcanoes** on **plywood boards.**

4

Bikers in **scuba gear** pedal along the **Atlantic Ocean's floor** for an **annual race** off the coast of North Carolina, U.S.A.

5

Skyaking involves athletes **parachuting** from a plane while **strapped to a kayak** and then landing on water.

6

Winter waves off Cape Peninsula, South Africa, can **swell to 25 feet** (7.6 m), attracting daredevil **surfers.**

7

Abraham Lincoln was an accomplished **wrestler.**

8

The average **life span** of an NBA basketball is about **10,000 bounces.**

9

In the 1800s, baseball **umpires** sat in **rocking chairs** behind **home plate.**

10

Figure skating was once part of the **Summer Olympics.**

Relieving Facts About Ridiculous Restrooms

1 A restroom stall in Japan is built inside an aquarium where fish and sea turtles swim by as you do your business.

2 A restroom in Mexico has a transparent glass floor so that you can see the 15-story drop below.

3 To find the bathroom at a restaurant in Milwaukee, Wisconsin, U.S.A., patrons must navigate through mazes and avoid a trick door.

4 You can find a historic two-story outhouse in a town in Illinois, U.S.A.

5

Astronauts on the International Space Station have to strap down their feet so they don't float away while using the bathroom.

6

Coca-Cola Park in Pennsylvania, U.S.A., has a gaming system in one of the restrooms.

7

There's a restaurant where guests sit on toilet seats and are served food on platters that look like mini toilets.

8

Australians celebrate Australia Day by racing "dunnies"—portable toilets on wheels.

9

Chongqing, China, is home to the world's largest public bathroom—the building has 1,000 toilets.

10

You can take a bath surrounded by elephants, giraffes, and other safari wildlife at Madikwe Hills Lodge in South Africa.

BUS DOES PUSH-UPS

WHAT Exercising sculpture

WHERE London, England

DETAILS This bus will get you pumped! Called the London Booster, the "muscular" double-decker was built in honor of the 2012 Summer Olympics in London. To create the installation, an artist fitted a real bus from the 1950s with electrical arms that move up and down, push-up style. Who knew buses could be bodybuilders?

Extreme Weirdness

WEAR YOUR LAWN

WHAT Grass-covered flip-flops

WHERE New South Wales Coast, Australia

DETAILS Want to feel the grass between your toes? Just plant your feet in these grass-topped flip-flops, designed to give you the sensation of being outdoors anytime. Don't worry about watering the sandals—the grass is actually a layer of artificial turf. You'll have some happy feet!

ZIPPER OPENS APARTMENT

WHAT Unzipped floor

WHERE Tokyo, Japan

DETAILS You won't keep your lips zipped about this display! Built into the floor of an apartment, the temporary art installation is shaped like a giant zipper that's opening up the floor. The zipper is made of wood, so it doesn't actually move. But the artist hopes you'll look twice before zipping by.

BIIIGGG BINOCULARS

WHAT Binocular-shaped entrance

WHERE Venice, California, U.S.A.

DETAILS Did somebody ask for a better view? Sculptors Claes Oldenburg and Coosje van Bruggen designed this 45-foot (13.7-m)-tall set of binoculars that now serves as an office entrance for Google. So that's what they mean by "internet search."

GIANT SILVERWARE

WHAT Super-large spoon

WHERE Seoul, South Korea

DETAILS Think how much cereal could fit on this spoon. World Vision, a charity that works to end poverty, set up the spoon as part of an exhibit to collect donations for children in need. Giant coins were placed with the huge silverware to represent the money needed to help. Big spoon, big coins—and big hearts.

POTATOES ON PARADE

WHAT Spud-shaped tricycles

WHERE Lima, Peru

DETAILS Can you say spud-tacular? Potato sellers marched in a parade with potato-shaped carts for National Potato Day—a celebration of this food that originated in South America. This annual festival also includes a potato market and competitions to create the best potato-based dishes.

Heroic Facts About Daring Dudes

1

Robbie Maddison is a famous motocross star who did a backflip while leaping over the opened Tower Bridge in London, England, in 2009.

2

Shakespeare is known as the greatest writer of the English language and coined more than 1,700 words that are still used today.

3

Alexander the Great was the king of Macedonia for 13 years and never lost a battle during his reign.

4

Chief Sitting Bull stood up to the U.S. government when it attempted to take over Lakota tribe land.

5

Charles Lindbergh was the first pilot to **fly nonstop** across the Atlantic Ocean.

6

Chesley "Sully" Sullenberger is a **pilot who safely landed a jetliner** carrying 155 people after the **engine failed.**

7

Harvey Milk helped pass a city ordinance in San Francisco, California, U.S.A., in 1978 that **outlawed discrimination** based on sexual orientation.

8

Bill Gates, the founder of **Microsoft,** donated $30 billion to form a foundation that works to **improve conditions** around the world.

9

Abraham Lincoln was president during the Civil War, during which he worked to keep the states together and helped **abolish slavery.**

10

Michael Jordan is considered the **world's greatest** basketball player—he led the Chicago Bulls to win **six championships** and took home five **MVP awards.**

Heroic Facts About Gutsy Gals

1

In 1979, Sylvia Earle took a walk 1,250 feet (381 m) below the surface of the **Pacific Ocean,** which set the record at the time for the **lowest depth** a human explored on foot.

2

Sabine Lisicki has the **fastest serve** in women's tennis, at **131 miles an hour!** (211 km/h)

3

For a long time, scientists believed that **humans** were the only animals **smart enough** to create their own **utensils for food,** but Jane Goodall discovered that **chimpanzees** also **use tools.**

4

Oprah Winfrey was born into **extreme poverty,** but she built a media empire worth **$4 billion** and is now one of the **richest people** in the U.S.

5

On June 18, 1983, Sally Ride became the **first American woman** and **the youngest** astronaut, at age 32, to **travel to space.**

6

At the 1988 Olympics in South Korea, Jackie Joyner-Kersee **won three golds, a silver, and two bronzes**—and at the time held the most medals of any woman in **Olympic track and field** history.

7

In 2015, **Misty Copeland** became the first African-American woman to be named a **principal dancer**—the highest level—in the 75-year history of the American Ballet Theatre.

8

Misty May-Treanor and Kerri Walsh Jennings **played volleyball** in **three different Olympics,** playing 43 sets and losing only one!

9

First Lady **Eleanor Roosevelt** spoke up for those who didn't have a voice, and, at a time when few married women **had a career, she matched** the president's yearly income.

10

Ada Lovelace, a mathematician who lived during the 1800s, was the **first computer programmer.**

What's the Difference?

Check out these similar pairings and see how you can determine this from that!

CLUB SODA VS. SPARKLING MINERAL WATER

These bubbly beverages are exciting to drink, but why drink one instead of the other? Club soda doesn't have naturally occurring bubbles—the bubbles are added in by way of minerals added to the water! It doesn't have a very strong flavor, which makes it ideal for mixing with other liquids to create your own bubbly concoction. On the other hand, sparkling mineral water usually comes from a natural spring or well and is naturally carbonated. The minerals in sparkling water can make for a bitter or intense taste.

TSUNAMI VS. TIDAL WAVE

These terrifying beasts of water are actually created by different forces. Tidal waves often occur in shallow water when a high tide rises so rapidly that a "wave" develops. They are created by weather and gravitational forces from the sun or moon. Some tidal waves can be as tall as 50 feet (15.2 m), while tsunamis may reach up to 100 feet (30.5 m) high. Tsunamis usually consist of multiple waves, not just one, with waves sometimes being an hour apart. Unlike tidal waves, tsunamis are not formed by gravitational forces, but more by water displacement and disturbances from events such as earthquakes or even erupting underwater volcanoes.

LLAMA VS. ALPACA

Both of these fluffy, long-necked buddies hail from South America. Llamas are roughly double the size of their smaller alpaca counterparts. Their ears are different shapes and lengths as well, with the llama's ears much taller than the alpaca's short and stubby ones. But despite their differences in size, alpacas produce much more fibrous fur compared to llamas. Llamas have been bred as a pack-carrying animal for thousands of years, whereas alpacas have been bred for just as long but specifically for their luxurious fiber. Plus, llamas have actually been used to guard alpacas!

PAPAYA VS. MANGO

Their shape might be similar, but take one bite and you'll notice the differences immediately! The mango tends to be much sweeter and firmer than a papaya. You can tell a mango is ripe by the golden yellow color on the inside. Papayas, on the other hand, are much milder in taste, though still sweet, and considerably mushier. A ripe papaya is distinguished by its dark orange color. There are dozens of tiny seeds at the center of a papaya that can be eaten, but beware, they have a bit of a spicy flavor and are sometimes used as a pepper replacement. Mangoes, on the other hand, have one large seed in the middle.

HAIR VS. FUR

Only mammals have hair, and fur in particular is hair on nonhuman mammals. Sounds like it's just the word itself that's the difference, right? Not so much. Fur comes with its own benefits. For animals, fur provides them with protection from temperature, whether hot or cold, and can also protect them from rain. Hair on humans does not help regulate body temperature to nearly the same extent, if at all. Human hair can also continue to grow, and we simply cut it when we feel it gets too long, whereas animal fur tends to stop at a certain length and then fall out to be replaced.

Alpaca

1

Virgin Islands National Park features a 225-yard (206-m)-long underwater snorkeling trail!

2

Skeleton Coast National Park in Namibia, Africa, is home to the remains of hundreds of shipwrecks.

3

Wood Buffalo National Park in Canada has the world's largest beaver dam—it's nearly nine times as long as the Statue of Liberty is tall.

4

The oldest human remains (2.8 million years old) were found in Serengeti National Park, Tanzania.

5

Great Smoky Mountains is the most visited national park in the United States.

6

The Yarlung Tsangpo Grand Canyon in the Himalaya is 17,000 feet (5,300 m) deep—that's three times deeper than the U.S.A.'s Grand Canyon.

7

Crater Lake, in Oregon, U.S.A., is 1,943 feet (592 m) deep, enough to hide 1.5 Empire State Buildings.

8

The longest cave system in the world is at Mammoth Cave National Park, Kentucky, U.S.A., where more than 405 miles (652 km) have been explored.

9

The Old Faithful geyser at Yellowstone National Park, Wyoming, U.S.A., can shoot out of the ground up to 184 feet. (56 m)

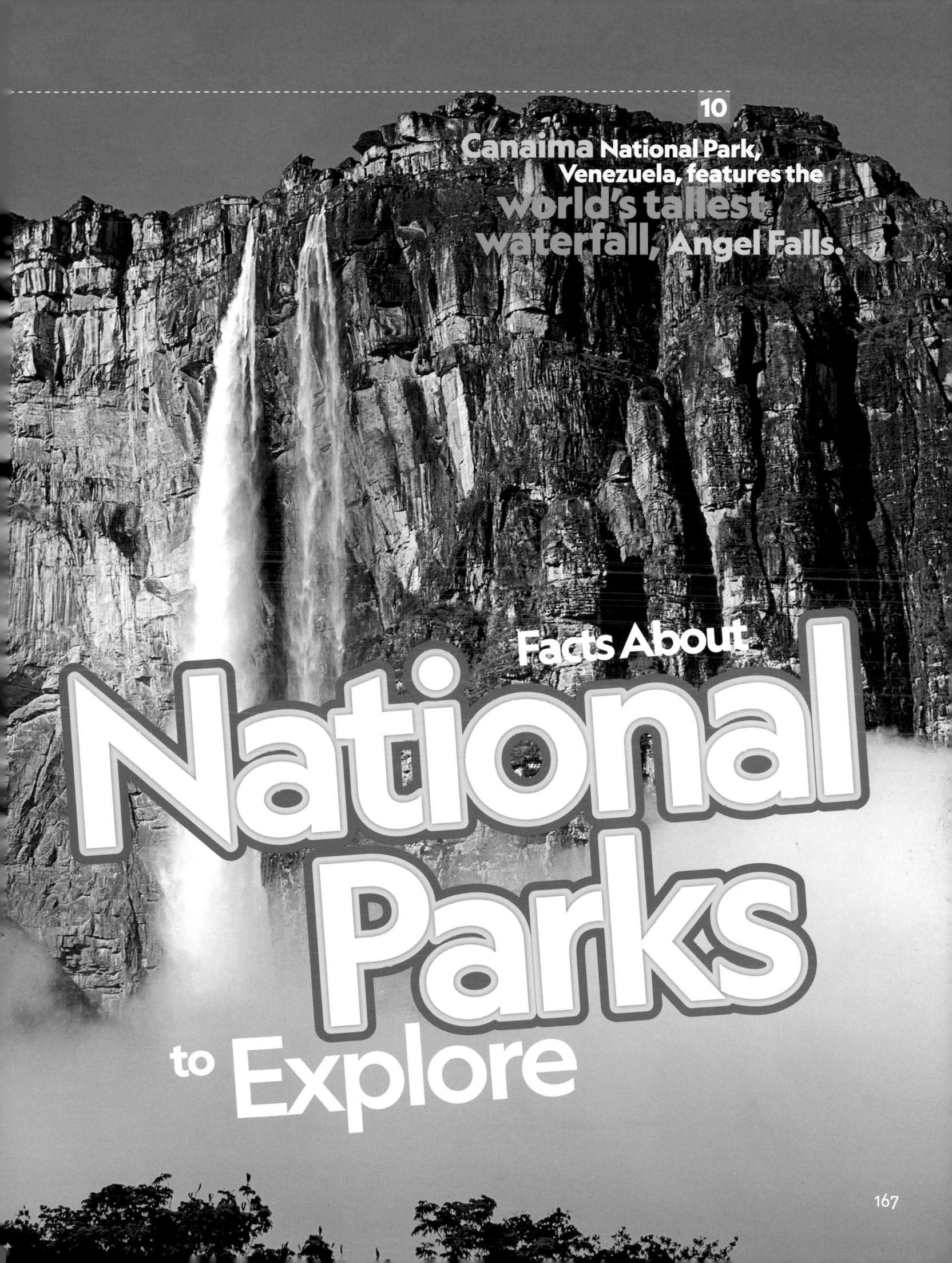

10

Canaima National Park, Venezuela, features the world's tallest waterfall, Angel Falls.

Facts About National Parks to Explore

Fierce Facts About Vikings

1

Viking boots were often made of goatskin.

2

A rare hoard of Viking treasure found in Scotland contained jewelry, armbands, brooches, and cross necklaces.

3

Vikings didn't wear horned helmets—that look was popularized by painters.

4

Distinguished Vikings were sometimes buried in ships that would be set on fire and pushed out to sea.

5

Vikings worshipped a god named Loki who could shape-shift into different animals.

6

Vikings enjoyed skiing and worshipped a skiing god named Ullr.

7

The name "Viking" means "a pirate raid" in Old Norse language.

8

Thursday is named after Thor, the Norse god of thunder.

9

Denmark is home to the Ladby ship, a ship burial of a Viking king that dates back to the year 925.

10

A group of Viking warriors called berserkers wore bear or wolf skins and howled in battle like wild animals.

Energetic Facts About Electricity

1

You're more likely to get a shock from static electricity in winter than in summer.

2

A platypus hunts using electrical impulses.

3

A Japanese aquarium once used an eel to power the lights on a Christmas tree.

4

The electricity in Albertville, France, is powered by cheese.

5

Only one percent of a microwave's time is used to heat food; the other 99 percent of the time it is in standby mode, using more electricity to power its clock than heating food.

6

There is a pedal-powered cinema in which a few people pedal bicycles to power an outdoor movie theater for up to 500 people.

7

Nearby lightning strikes can cause some mushrooms to multiply and grow in size in the wild.

8

The Oriental hornet traps sunlight in its "skin" and turns it into electricity.

9

Muscle cells in the heart contract due to electricity that runs through your body.

10

Sharks can detect electric fields thanks to the thousands of tiny pores on their heads that are filled with an electrically conductive jelly.

The Dumbo octopus is known for its adorable elephant-like ears and is the world's deepest-living octopus species,

some living as deep as

23,000 feet (7,000 m)
below sea level.

Futuristic Facts About Technology

1

The Int-Ball is an **adorable drone,** slightly larger than a softball, **that floats** through space on its own or can be **remote-controlled from Earth.**

2

The Weird Hotel in Japan is **staffed almost totally by robots,** including a **dinosaur robot** receptionist that checks you in.

3

Dobi Robots broke a world record for the **largest number** of **robots dancing** at the same time: **1,069.**

4

Harry the **robot** knows **how to play the trumpet.**

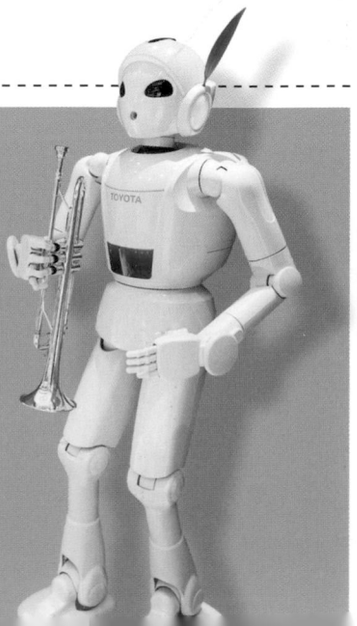

A music-performing **band of robots** called Z-Machines has a guitarist with **78 fingers** and a drummer with **22 arms.**

5

Robear is a **robot nurse** with the **face of a bear** that helps care for patients by **lifting them** out of bed into a wheelchair.

6

Researchers **study geckos** to learn how to **help robots** and **astronauts** maneuver around space structures.

8

7

Russia once **built a computer** powered by **water.**

9

There is a **Rubik's Cube robot** that can **solve itself.**

10

The world's **largest walking robot** is a **dragon** measuring 51 feet 6 inches (15.7 m) long and 26 feet 10 inches (8.2 m) tall that can **blow flames.**

1

Like humans, monkeys do not **eat the skins** of **bananas**; they **peel them** open!

2

Monkeys **groom each other** not only to get rid of dirt and parasites, but also to show **affection** toward one another.

3

At Jigokudani Monkey Park in Japan, **snow monkeys** bathe in natural **hot springs** during the winter.

4

The howls of **howler monkeys** can be heard up to **three miles** (5 km) **away.**

5

You can tell **how healthy** a bald uakari is by the **shade of red** on its face.

6

Monkeys have tails, but apes do not.

7

Capuchin monkeys are often trained to **assist people** who have lost movement in their body to do **helpful tasks** like turning **light switches** on and off.

8

Brazil is home to more than **50 species** of monkeys—that's more than **any other country** in the world!

9

One man paid **$25,000** for a collection of **paintings by a chimpanzee.**

10

When the beloved children's book character **Curious George** debuted in the United Kingdom, **his name** was changed to **Zozo.**

Playful Facts to Monkey Around With

Amazing Facts About Roadside Attractions

1

Check out a giant **dragon statue** made completely out of **porcelain dishware** in Yangzhou, China!

2

The walls in **Bubblegum Alley** in California, U.S.A., are covered in **20 years'** worth of **chewed gum.**

3

You can **visit a house** in Headington, England, that has a sculpture on the roof of a **giant shark** diving into the attic.

4

The world's **smallest church** is in New York, U.S.A., in the **middle of a pond.**

5

Visit **Larry the Lobster** in Kingston South East, Australia, where he stands at **56 feet** (17 m) tall.

6 Riders can **wait for the bus** inside a **strawberry** or other **fruit-shaped bus stops** in Konagai, Japan.

7 There's a **watchtower** in Colorado, U.S.A., with a nearby gift shop **shaped like a UFO.**

8 There is a **Ouija board tombstone** in a cemetery in Maryland, U.S.A., for the man who **patented** the board.

9 **Take a drive** on the **Enchanted Highway** in North Dakota, U.S.A., where you can see sculptures of **giant grasshoppers.**

10 **When it snows** in Minneapolis, Minnesota, U.S.A., a massive sculpture of a **spoon and cherry** looks like the world's largest **sundae.**

Giraffes and humans have the same number of bones in their necks:

7.

Behind the Facts

We're sure you're wondering how we got so many awesome facts about so many awesome topics into this book. First, we came up with a list of all the coolest and most interesting things out there—things we know kids want to know more about. Like wild and wacky animals and strange things about space. Caves, chocolate, and birds. Amusement parks. Slime. Baby animals. All kinds of stuff. Then we found 10 or 20 of the most exciting and surprising facts about those topics to arrange on each page. We carefully researched each and every fact to make sure it's absolutely true ... then we packed it full of cool bonus content! Things like strange places, moments of extreme weirdness around the world, and a feature called "What's the Difference?" that will answer age-old questions like "What's the difference between a kangaroo and a wallaby?" And we designed the pages so colorfully that you'll never get bored looking at them and will love flipping to all your favorite parts. Bet you didn't know who worked to make this book! It took a group of writers, editors, photo editors, and designers—the greatest book team around!

Illustration Credits

ASP: Alamy Stock Photo; DT: Dreamstime; GI: Getty Images; SS: Shutterstock

Cover (sloth), Vilainecrevette/DT; (black hole), Photo Researchers/Science History Images/ASP; (dolphin), Andrea Izzotti/iStockphoto/GI; (orange slices), Albo003/SS; (bristlecone pine tree), Tomas Tichy/SS; (pink flamingo feathers), Jak Wonderly/NGK; (tourmaline), Bildagentur Zoonar GmbH/SS; (gold statuette), Kenneth Garrett/National Geographic Creative; (Moais statues on Easter Island), Viktorus/DT; (llama), Jose A. Bernat Bacete/Moment RF/GI; (strawberries), Denis Larkin/SS; (blue macaw feathers), Juniors Bildarchiv GmbH/SS;(piano keys), Vorobyeva/SS; back cover (zebra finches), Giel, O/ASP; (fingerprints), Andrey Kuzmin/SS; (Jack Russell terrier), Eric Isselee/SS; (chameleon), Cathy Keifer/SS; spine (lightning), Anna Om/SS; 1 (BACKGROUND), Mitsuyoshi Tatematsu/Nature Production/Minden Pictures; 2-3 (BACKGROUND), Inge Johnsson/ASP; 4 (UP), Kateryna Kon/SS; 4 (alpaca), fotobook/SS; 4 (lightning), James Insogna/DT; 4 (LO), Ljupco Smokovski/SS; 5 (UP), CB2/ZOB/Supplied by WENN/Newscom; 5 (Parthenon), PNIK/SS; 5 (petri dish), Per Bengtsson/SS; 5 (LO), Robert Eastman/SS; 6-7 (BACKGROUND), Pefkos/SS; 6 (UP), Greg and Jan Ritchie/SS; 6 (LO), National Geographic/David Liittschwager/GI; 7 (LE), Morozova Anna/SS; 7 (RT), Eric Isselee/SS; 8 (UP LE), Michael Flippo/ASP; 8 (UP RT), vitaliy_73/SS; 8 (CTR), Jeremy Pembrey/ASP; 8 (LO LE), Thom Lang/GI; 8 (LO RT), Richard Bord/GI; 9 (UP), Rick Madonik/Toronto Star/GI; 9 (CTR LE), Richard G. Bingham II/ASP; 9 (LO LE), Kuttelvaserova Stuchelova/SS; 9 (LO RT), Zhang Weiqing - CNImaging/Newscom; 10-11 (BACKGROUND), Dmitry Pustovalov/SS; 11 (UP RT), Jannarong/SS; 11 (LO LE), Andrea Danti/SS; 11 (LO RT), JoeFotoSS/SS; 12 (UP), fotobook/SS; 12 (CTR), Franco Tempesta; 12 (LO), khai9000/iStock/GI; 13 (UP), Eric Isselee/SS; 13 (CTR), Andrew Burgess/SS; 13 (LO), Junial Enterprises/SS; 14 (UP), Richard Whitcombe/SS; 14 (UP LE), Margot Sheridan/DT; 14 (CTR RT), bonchan/SS; 14 (LO CTR LE), NooMUboN Photo/SS; 14 (LO), Binh Thanh Bui/SS; 15 (BACKGROUND), David Nunuk/Science Photo Library/GI; 16 (UP LE), Tsekhmister/SS; 16 (UP RT), Fotorola/ASP; 16 (CTR), Dani Vincek/SS; 16 (LO), Bazzano Photography/ASP; 17 (UP), Brum/SS; 17 (CTR), Africa Studio/SS; 17 (LO LE), MidoSemsem/SS; 17 (LO RT), Morley Read/ASP; 18-19 (BACKGROUND), Tom Till/ASP; 18 (LO), NASA/STEREO/Helioviewer; 19 (UP LE), rvlsoft/SS; 19 (UP RT), Markus Loretto/SS; 19 (LO), S.E.A. Photo/ASP; 20 (UP), kosam/SS; 20 (CTR LE), Anton Starikov/DT; 20 (LO RT), Steven R Smith/SS; 21 (LE), Guiziou Franck/hemis.fr/ASP; 21 (CTR), Cara-Foto/SS; 21 (RT), cinoby/iStock; 22 (LE), joyfull/SS; 22 (RT), A & J Visage/ASP; 23 (UP), The Natural History Museum/ASP; 23 (LO LE), ZQFotography/SS; 23 (LO RT), Fekete Tibor/SS; 24-25 (BACKGROUND), Andrey Nekrasov/ASP; 24 (UP), fivespots/SS; 24 (CTR), MN84/SS; 24 (LO), Besjunior/ASP; 25 (UP), Maridav/SS; 25 (LO), National Geographic/Joel Sartore/GI; 26-27 (BACKGROUND), Kateryna Kon/SS; 26 (UP LE),), Kateryna Kon/SS; 26 (UP RT), ramcreations/SS; 26 (LO LE), mayakova/SS; 26 (LO RT), Mega Pixel/SS; 27 (UP), mb123/SS; 27 (LE), Handmade Pictures/ASP; 27 (RT), Per Bengtsson/SS; 28-29 (BACKGROUND), S.Rohrlach/SS; 30-31 (BACKGROUND), Rafal Szozda/SS; 30 (UP), California Academy of Sciences/Science Source; 30 (LO), Ian Dyball/SS; 31 (UP), Tuangtong Soraprasert/SS; 32 (UP), The Print Collector Heritage Images/Newscom; 33 (UP), mauritius images GmbH/ASP; 33 (LO LE), DEA Picture Library/De Agostini/GI; 33 (LO RT), Jeff Pachoud/Stringer/GI; 34 (UP LE), Atiketta Sangasaeng/SS; 34 (UP CTR), Isselee/DT; 34 (UP RT), AP Photo/Kyodo News; 35 (UP), Proceedings of the National Academy of Sciences/PNAS; 35 (LO LE), Nicky Bay Photography; 35 (LO RT), Denis Radovanovic/SS; 36-37 (BACKGROUND), Hriana/SS; 37 (UP), Swapan Photography/SS; 37 (CTR LE), Tim UR/SS; 37 (CTR RT), Cultura RM/ASP; 37 (LO), Jackan/SS; 38 (UP), Maximilian Stock Ltd./GI; 38 (LO), Liliya Kulianionak/SS; 39 (UP), Geri Lavrov/GI; 39 (CTR LE), chengyuzheng/iStock; 39 (CTR RT), Jorge Santos/age fotostock RM/GI; 39 (LO LE), Fred Stein Archive/GI; 39 (LO RT), Peter Dazele/GI; 40 (UP), Bruce Corbett/ASP; 40 (LO), All Canada Photos/ASP; 41 (BACKGROUND), Gunter Marx/HI/ASP; 42 (LE), Cultural Archive/ASP; 42 (RT), Citizen of the Planet/ASP; 43 (LE), Daniel M. Cisilino/DT; 43 (RT), GL Archive/ASP; 43 (LO), Sabena Jane Blackbird/ASP; 44-45 (BACKGROUND), MaRabelo/iStock/GI; 44 (UP), Alexander Shalamov/DT; 44 (LO), Brandon Rosenblum/GI; 45 (LO), jakkrit pimpru/SS; 46-47 (BACKGROUND), Borna_Mirahmadian/SS; 46 (LO), David Hagerman/iStock/GI;

47 (UP), Timur Kulgarin/SS; 47 (LO), Art Media Heritage Images/Newscom; 48-49 (BACKGROUND), dottedhippo/iStock; 48 (UP LE), NASA/World History Archive & ARPL/ASP; 48 (UP CTR), Oksun70/DT; 48 (UP RT), Oksun70/DT; 48 (CTR), Andreykuzmin/DT; 48 (LO), NASA's Goddard Space Flight Center/NAOJ; 49 (UP), Marc Ward/SS; 50 (UP LE), Joel Arem/GI; 50 (UP RT), Andreas Strauss/LOOK Die Bildagentur der Fotografen GmbH/ASP; 50 (CTR), DWithers/iStock; 50 (LO LE), Phil Degginger/ASP; 50 (LO RT), ODM/SS; 51 (UP), Bildagentur Zoonar GmbH/SS; 51 (CTR), Ingemar Magnusson/DT; 51 (LO), Mikel Bilbao/age fotostock; 52-53 (BACKGROUND), Christian Roberts-Olsen/SS; 52 (UP), David McNew/Stringer/GI; 53 (UP), NinaM/SS; 53 (LO), Vasili's Ververidis/DT; 54 (BACKGROUND), Bucha Natallia/SS; 55 (UP), Xinhua/ASP; 55 (CTR LE), ZJAN/Canadian Tire Corporation/WENN/Newscom; 55 (CTR RT), Bimal Gautam/Xinhua/ASP; 55 (LO LE), Jonathan Hordle/Barcroft Media/GI; 55 (LO RT), Stringer/Mexico/Reuters/Newscom; 56-57 (BACKGROUND), B Brown/SS; 56 (UP), ruzanna/SS; 56 (LO), Daniela Duncan/GI; 57 (LO), Sofiaworld/SS; 58 (UP LE), Hayati Kayhan/SS; 58 (UP RT), Michelle Patrick/SS; 58 (LO), karen roach/SS; 59 (UP), Richard Watkins/ASP; 59 (LO LE), xavier gallego morell/SS; 59 (LO RT), Natali Zakharova/SS; 60 (LE), Brian A Jackson/SS; 60 (RT), siriratsavett/SS; 61 (LO LE), TCassidy/iStock; 61 (CTR), Dan Kosmayer/SS; 61 (LO RT), CB2/ZOB/WENN/Newscom; 62-63 (BACKGROUND), Irina Dmitrienko/ASP; 62 (LE), PNIK/SS; 62 (RT), Photo of Adorant Don Hitchcock; 63 (LE), Yurumi/SS; 63 (RT), Photo Researchers/Science History Images/ASP; 64 (UP), FoodPhotogr Eising/Bon Appetit/ASP; 64 (LO), Liz Melchor; 65 (UP LE), Fuse/GI; 65 (UP RT), Industry Kitchen; 65 (LO), Feng Yu/DT; 66 (UP), mawear/iStock; 66 (CTR LE), Sarah2/SS; 66 (CTR RT), vnlit/SS; 66 (LO LE), Ellen van Bodegom/GI; 66 (LO RT), RichardSeeley/iStock; 67 (UP), blickwinkel/ASP; 67 (CTR LE), Nella/SS; 67 (CTR RT), Ondrej Prosicky/SS; 67 (LO), mlorenz/SS; 68 (UP), Hector Ruiz Villar/SS; 68 (CTR LE), Oleksandrum/SS; 68 (CTR RT), Cameron Rutt/GI; 68 (LO LE), monticello/SS; 68 (LO RT), Picture by Tambako the Jaguar/GI; 69 (BACKGROUND), Alex Mustard/Nature Picture Library/GI; 70-71 (BACKGROUND), M Swiet Productions/GI; 70 (UP), Sorin Colac/DT.com; 70 (LO), David Aguilar/NGS; 71 (UP), Tetra Images/age fotostock; 71 (LO), Roman Barelko/ASP; 72-73 (BACKGROUND), DPK-Photo/ASP; 72 (UP), Michael Elliott/DT; 72 (LO), Maciej Bledowski/SS; 73 (UP), George H.H. Huey/ASP; 73 (LO), Carl & Ann Purcell/GI; 74 (LO), Kemphoto artistic works/ASP; 74-75 (BACKGROUND), Willyam Bradberry/SS; 74 (UP), mikeledray/SS; 75 (UP), Michael Szönyi/ASP; 76 (UP LE), Tui De Roy/Minden Pictures; 76 (UP RT), Michel Gunther/BIOSPHOTO/ASP; 76 (LO), Andrew Burgess/SS; 77 (UP), Visuals Unlimited, Inc./Joe McDonald/GI; 77 (CTR), amwu/iStock; 77 (LO LE), Lunamarina/DT; 77 (LO RT), Isselee/DT; 78-79 (BACKGROUND), martellostudio/SS; 78 (UP), Historical/Corbis/GI; 79 (LE), Irochka/DT; 79 (RT), Sergey Skleznev/SS; 80-81 (BACKGROUND), Thoai Pham/ASP; 80 (UP), golubka57/SS; 80 (CTR), Danita Delimont/GI; 80 (LO), Nicky Bay Photography; 82 (UP), ARTSILENSE/SS; 82 (LO), lostinbids/GI; 83 (UP RT), haveseen/SS; 83 (CTR LE), stockshoppe/SS; 83 (CTR RT), PeopleImages/iStock/GI; 83 (LO), Seb Oliver/age fotostock; 84-85 (BACKGROUND), Brent Stephenson/Nature Picture Library; 84 (UP), Lorenzo Mattei/ASP; 84 (LO), Eric Isselee/SS; 85 (UP), Maudib/iStock; 85 (LO), Ilya Akinshin/SS; 86-87 (BACKGROUND), Henk Meijer/ASP; 88 (UP LE), Artokoloro Quint Lox Limited/ASP; 88 (UP RT), Chamille White/SS; 88 (UP CTR), Science & Society Picture Library/GI; 88 (LO LE), NASA; 88 (LO RT), Art Collection 4/ASP; 89 (UP), Library of Congress; 89 (LO), Khomulo Anna/SS; 90-91 (BACKGROUND), Yevhenii Chulovskyi/SS; 90 (UP), Alex Hyde/Nature Picture Library; 91 (UP), Ito Fukuo/Minden Pictures; 91 (LO LE), blickwinkel/Kaufung/ASP; 91 (LO RT), Ermolaev Alexander/SS; 92-93 (BACKGROUND), J. Helgason/SS; 92 (LO), pio3/SS; 93 (UP), Jonathan Blair/GI; 93 (CTR), Andrey Pavlov/SS; 93 (LO LE), Talvi/SS; 93 (LO RT), Mattes RenÃ/GI; 94 (UP), Stephen Alvarez/GI; 94 (LO), Corbin17/ASP; 95 (BACKGROUND), Yann Arthus-Bertrand/GI; 96 (UP), DenisNata/SS; 96 (LO RT), kramikel/iStock; 96 (LO), Eric Isselee/SS; 97 (UP), Noella Ballenger/ASP; 97 (CTR RT), larus/SS; 97 (LO LE), tkemot/SS; 97 (LO RT), Wang LiQiang/SS; 98-99 (UP LE), Life On White/GI; 98 (UP LE), Federicoriz/DT; 98 (UP RT), Ingram; 98 (LO), pjmalsbury/iStock; 99 (UP), imageBROKER/ASP; 99 (CTR), FineShine/SS; 99 (LO), AP Photo/FOTOPRESS, Ross Land; 100-101 (BACKGROUND), TRphotos/SS; 100 (LO), Alain Denantes/Gamma-Rapho/GI; 101 (UP LE), AppleZoomZoom/SS; 101 (UP RT), Atlantis Bahamas; 102-103 (BACKGROUND), Anna Kucherova/SS; 102 (UP), Mark Moffett/Minden Pictures/GI; 102 (CTR), kikkerdirk/iStock; 102 (LO), Paul R. Sterry/Nature Photographers Ltd/ASP; 103 (LO), Richard Merritt FRPS/GI; 104 (UP LE), Andy Crawford/GI; 104 (UP RT), Carl Fischer Music/Jay Berger; 105 (LE), Rick Findler/PA Images/ASP; 105 (CTR), paffy/SS; 105 (RT), Soranome/SS; 106 (UP), Petras Malukas/AFP/GI; 106 (UP CTR LE), Ben Birchall/PA Images/ASP; 106 (UP CTR RT), Tony Farrugia/ASP; 106 (LO LE), Raul Arboleda/AFP/Stringer/GI; 106 (LO RT), Solent News/Splash News/Newscom; 107 (BACKGROUND), Reuters/Danny Moloshok; 108 (UP LE), Melinda Fawver/SS; 108 (UP RT), Ishay Botbol/ASP; 108 (LO), Ismailciydem/iStock; 109 (UP), imageBROKER/Marko König/ASP; 109 (CTR), Andrew Calverley/DT; 109 (LO), Betty Gillis; 110 (UP), Ultrashock/SS; 110 (LO), Lian van den Heever/GI; 111 (UP LE), Ichiro Katakai/GI; 111 (UP RT), Jody Ann/SS; 111 (CTR LE), F. Hecker/picture alliance/blickwinkel/F/Newscom; 111 (CTR RT), autsawin uttisin/SS; 111 (LO), Jens Peter/EyeEm/GI; 112-113 (BACKGROUND), Paul Nicklen/GI; 112 (UP), Martin Harvey/ASP; 112 (LO LE), Sylvain Cordier/BIOSPHOTO/ASP; 112 (LO RT), M. Ohl/Musuem für Naturkunde Berlin; 113 (UP), Michael Breuer/GI; 113 (LO), David Yeo/GI; 114 (BACKGROUND), Ljupco Smokovski/SS; 115 (UP), Littlekidmoment/SS; 115 (LO LE), The Washington Post/GI; 115 (LO RT), fergregory/iStock; 116 (LE), Yellow Cat/SS; 116 (CTR), susan.k./GI; 116 (RT), Gossip/SS; 117 (UP), EtiAmmos/SS; 117 (LE), CareyHope/iStock; 117 (RT), New Africa/SS; 117 (LO), Popperfoto/GI; 118-119 (BACKGROUND), Caiaimage/Chris Ryan/GI; 119 (UP), ronstik/SS; 119 (LO LE), Howard Davis Datel; 119 (LO RT), Valentyn Volkov/SS; 120 (UP LE), Halfdark/GI; 120 (UP RT), juliedeshaies/iStock; 120 (LO), Ashley Landis/ZUMA Press, Inc./ASP; 121 (UP LE), Boonchuay1970's/SS; 121 (UP RT), Hinterhaus Productions/GI; 121 (CTR LE), Tono Balaguer/SS; 121 (CTR RT), Pipa100/DT; 121 (LO LE), Maks Narodenko/SS; 121 (LO RT), Eaglesky/SS; 122-123 (BACKGROUND), den-belitsky/iStock; 122 (UP LE), Simon Montgomery/robertharding/ASP; 122 (UP RT), patti jean images and designs by patti jean guerrero/SS; 122 (LO), LanaG/ASP; 123 (UP), Ellen Creager/MCT/Newscom; 124 (UP), kiv_ph/SS; 124 (CTR), Nadezhda V. Kulagina/SS; 124 (LO), Lam Yik Fei/GI; 125 (UP), Jennifer Booher/ASP; 125 (CTR), Kyselova Inna/SS; 125 (LO), gnomish/Stockimo/ASP; 126-127 (BACKGROUND), Michael Nolan/robertharding/ASP; 126 (UP), Vladimir Zadvinskii/SS; 126 (LO LE), GL Archive/ASP; 126 (LO RT), Historic Collection/ASP; 128 (BACKGROUND), Oskar Franklin/DT; 129 (UP), IanDagnall Computing/ASP; 129 (CTR LE), Maks Narodenko/SS; 129 (CTR RT), Vlue/DT; 129 (LO LE), Yohei Osada/AFLO SPORT/Alamy Live/ASP; 129 (LO RT), Reinhard Hölzl/imageBROKER/ASP; 130 (UP), Tony Hassini International Magicians Society; 130 (LO), dragon_fang/SS; 130 (CTR), Taalvi/iStock; 131 (UP), Trinity Mirror/Mirrorpix/ASP; 131 (LO), Syda Productions/SS; 132-133 (BACKGROUND), Jimmy Chin/National Geographic Image Collection; 132 (UP), Colin Monteath/age fotostock/ASP; 132 (LO), Hulton Archive/Stringer/GI; 133 (LO RT), paul abbitt rml/ASP; 133 (UP), Dzmitry Kliapitski/ASP; 134 (UP), C&T/Bournemouth News/REX/SS; 134 (CTR LE), Granger.com - All rights reserved; 134 (CTR RT), Carlos Yudica/SS; 134 (LO), AP Photo/Dave Thompson/PA Wire; 135 (UP LE), Central Intelligence Agency; 135 (UP RT), paffy/SS; 135 (CTR), Jens Benninghofen/ASP; 135 (LO LE), Central Intelligence Agency; 135 (LO RT), Gerald S. Williams/KRT/Newscom; 136-137 (BACKGROUND), Jak Wonderly/NGK; 136 (UP), Melica/SS; 137 (CTR), Vaeenma/DT; 137 (LO LE), Reinhard Dirscherl/GI; 137 (LO RT), Trevor Marshall; 138 (LE), Four Oaks/SS; 138 (RT), Pegaz/ASP; 139 (UP LE), Ink Drop/SS; 139 (UP RT), GlobalP/iStock; 139 (LO), Thiti Sukapan/SS; 140-141 (BACKGROUND), Praisaeng/SS; 140 (UP), Rolf Nussbaumer/Minden Pictures; 140 (CTR LE), Cyril Ruoso/Minden Pictures/GI; 140 (CTR RT), Mitsuyoshi Tatematsu/Nature Production/Minden Pictures; 140 (LO), Austin Hargrave/Barcroft Media/GI; 142 (LE), ZUMA Press, Inc./ASP; 142 (RT), Luis Javier Sandoval Alvarado/RGB Ventures/SuperStock/ASP; 143 (UP LE), Suzanne Tucker/SS; 143 (UP RT), Richard Peterson/SS; 143 (CTR LE), Ploychan Lompong/SS; 143 (CTR CTR), Eillen/SS; 143 (CTR RT), Margo Harrison/SS; 143 (LO LE), Copyright by Orren Jack Turner, Princeton, N.J./Library of Congress; 143 (LO RT), Franck Fotos/ASP; 144 (LO), Michael Scheja/ASP; 145 (BACKGROUND), Razvan Ciuca/GI; 146-147 (BACKGROUND), Joanne Paquette; 146 (UP), Dale Darwin/Science Source/GI; 146 (LO), GI; 147 (UP), Runk/Schoenberger/Grant Heilman Photography/ASP; 147 (LO), Matthew Williams-Ellis/robertharding/ASP; 148 (UP LE), Suzi Eszterhas/Minden Pictures/GI; 148 (UP RT), Artoorek/DT; 148 (CTR), Gerry Yardy/ASP; 148 (LO), Heather LaVelle/SS; 149 (UP), Jason L. Price/SS; 149 (RT), Steve Byland/DT; 149 (LE), Best dog photo/SS; 150-151 (BACKGROUND), Paul Nicklen/National Geographic Image Collection; 150 (UP RT), Circa Images/Glasshouse Images/Alamy; 150 (LO), Eric Isselee/SS; 150 (UP LE), Byrdyak/iStock; 151 (RT), John Henshall/ASP; 152 (UP LE), danbreckwoldt/iStock; 152 (UP RT), Mike Windle/GI; 152 (LO LE), umnola/SS; 152 (LO RT), Solent News/Splash News/Newscom; 153 (UP LE), Ruaridh Connellan/Barcroft USA/Barcroft Media/GI; 153 (UP RT), Kathleen Howell/DT.com; 153 (CTR), Bettmann/GI; 153 (LO), posh puppy boutique; 154-155 (BACKGROUND), Caters News Agency; 154 (UP), Heikki Saukkomaa/AFP/GI155 (UP), Jeong Woo Kim/EyeEm/GI; 155 (LO LE), Issarawat Tattong/SS; 155 (LO RT), Kyodo News/GI; 156-157 (BACKGROUND), Madikwe Hills by Seasons in Africa; 156 (LO LE), Hernandez Silva Arquitectos; 156 (LO RT), Dylan Higgins; 157 (UP), Roger Ressmeyer/Corbis/VCG/GI; 157 (LO), Quirky China News/REX/SS/Rex Features; 158 (BACKGROUND), Sergey_Bogomyako/SS; 159 (LO LE), Jo Yong-Hak/Reuters/Newscom; 159 (UP), kkong/ASP; 159 (CTR LE), CB2/ZOB/WENN.com/Newscom; 159 (CTR RT), nik wheele/GI; 159 (LO RT), Luis Camacho Xinhua News Agency/Newscom; 160 (UP LE), Paul Fenton/ZUMA Press/ASP; 160 (UP RT), Ann Ronan Pictures/Print Collector/GI; 160 (LO), Library of Congress; 161 (LE), Library of Congress; 161 (RT), PCN Black/PCN Photography/ASP; 162 (LE), John B. Carnett/Bonnier Corp./GI; 162 (RT), Jensen Sutta/ASP; 163 (UP), Library of Congress; 163 (LO LE), NASA Photo/ASP; 163 (LO RT), Archivart/ASP; 164 (UP), Jari/iStock; 164 (CTR LE), SuperStock/age fotostock; 164 (CTR RT), Ingram Publishing/Newscom; 164 (LO LE), Seksun Guntanid/SS; 164 (LO RT), GlobalP/iStock; 165 (BACKGROUND), Spaces Images Blend Images/Newscom; 166-167 (BACKGROUND), David Woodfall/Avalon/Photoshot License/ASP; 166 (UP), imageBROKER/ASP; 166 (LO), f11photo/SS; 168-169 (BACKGROUND), Fernando G. Baptista/National Geographic Image Collection; 169 (UP LE), Graham Mulrooney/ASP; 169 (UP RT), The History Collection/ASP; 169 (LO LE), INTERFOTO History/ASP; 169 (LO RT), LifetimeStock/SS; 170 (UP LE), Science Photo Library; 170 (UP RT), Dave Watts/Nature Picture Library/GI; 170 (LO), Smileus/SS; 171 (UP), James Insogna/DT; 171 (UP CTR LE), Natalya Aksenova/DT; 171 (UP CTR RT), Dirk Ercken/DT; 171 (CTR LE), Colin Tonks; 171 (CTR RT), akiyoko/SS; 171 (LO), Michael Pitts/Bluegreen Pictures/ASP; 172-173 (BACKGROUND), Dante Fenolio/Science Source; 174 (UP LE), JAXA, ISS, NASA; 174 (UP RT), Nippon News/Aflo Co. Ltd./ASP; 174 (LO), Photo Japan/ASP; 175 (UP LE), Christopher Jue/Nippon News/Aflo Co. Ltd./ASP; 175 (UP RT), The Asahi Shimbun/GI; 175 (CTR LE), Ger Bosma/ASP; 175 (CTR RT), r.kathesi/SS; 175 (LO LE), Makstorm/SS; 175 (LO RT), CB2/ZOB/Supplied by WENN/Newscom; 176 (UP), Christian Hütter/imageBROKER/age fotostock; 176 (CTR), Morales/age fotostock; 176 (LO), Jeff Rotman/GI; 176-177 (BACKGROUND), Tier Und Naturfotografie J und C Sohns/GI; 178-179 (BACKGROUND), Colin Underhill/ASP; 178 (LO), Jack Grieve/ASP; 179 (UP), John S Lander/LightRocket/GI; 179 (LO), Franck Fotos/ASP; 180-181 (BACKGROUND), Sudhir Misra/EyeEm/GI

Index

Boldface indicates illustrations.

A

African lungfish 24
Águeda, Portugal 54, **54**
Air guitar 125, **125**
Alcatraz, California, U.S.A. 122
Alexander the Great 160, **160**
Ali, Muhammad 131, **131**
Alpacas 148, **148,** 164, **165**
Amusement parks 190–191
Angel Falls, Venezuela **166–167,** 167
Anglerfish 146
Anole lizards 77, **77**
Antarctica 80, 93, 108
Ants 17, **17,** 80, 93, **93,** 111, **111**
Apes 139, 176; *see also* Chimpanzees; Gorillas; Orangutans
Apollo 9 58
Apples 120
Aquariums 55, **55,** 156, 170
Arctic regions 84–85, **84–85**
Arms and armor 42–43, **42–43,** 125
Arsenic 8, **8**
Astronauts 9, 21, 48, 58, 78, 88, **88,** 157, 175; *see also* Ride, Sally
Atacama Desert, Chile 73
Australia
  coal fire 53
  crocodile swim 101
  lobster sculpture 178, **178**
  sprinkles 116
  toilet race 157
  wind instruments 104
  see also Jervis Bay

B

Babies 6, 82, **82**
Babirusas 112
Baby animals 7, **7,** 148–149, **148–149**
Bald uakaris 176, **176**
Ballet 163
Balloons 55, **55, 56–57,** 57, 126
Bananas
  as berries 120
  peeled by monkeys 176
  vs. plantains 129
  wild vs. farmed 37
Banjos 122, **122**
Baobab trees 95
Barbados, West Indies 123
Baseball 155
Basilisk lizards 77, **77**
Basketball
  ball life span 155
  players 79, 161, **161**
  polo and 154
Bathtubs
  for dogs 153, **153**
  gold 34, **34**
  outdoor **156–157,** 157
Bats 68, 140
Bears **85,** 150–151, **150–151**
Beaver dam, world's largest 166
Beavers 111, **111**
Bee orchids 66, **66**
Bees 11, **11,** 66, **66,** 84, 110, **110,** 150
Bigfoot 126, 142
Binocular-shaped entrance 159, **159**
Bioluminescence 146–147, **146–147**
Birds 30–31, **30–31,** 149, **149**
Birthdays 38, **38,** 114–117
Black sapote fruit 121, **121**
Blaine, David 130
Blind people 6
Blue cheese 17, **17**
Blue dragons (sea slugs) **28–29,** 29
Blue jays 66
Blue-ringed octopuses 103, **103**
Blue whales 149
Bobtail squid 146, **146**
Boomerang Nebula 48
Brain, human
  chemicals 7
  dreaming 82
  laughter 139
  theta waves 11
Brazil
  coins 62
  monkeys 176
  snakes 102
Brooches 9, 168
Bubblegum 59, **59**
Bubblegum Alley, California, U.S.A. 178
Bumblebee bats 140
Bun Scrambling Competition 124
Burrowing owls 66, **66**
Burrs 37
Bus sculpture 158, **158**
Bus stops, fruit-shaped 179, **179**
Butterflies 80–81, **80–81**

C

Canada
  Arctic territory 84
  beaver dam 166
  birthday traditions 117
  truck made of ice 55, **55**
  see also Northwest Territories; Spotted Lake

Canaima National Park, Venezuela **166–167,** 167
Candy 58–61, **58–61**; *see also* Chocolate
Capuchin monkeys 176, **176**
Caribou 40, **40**
Carrots 105, **105,** 121, **121**
Cars 106, **106,** 118–119, **118–119,** 152, **152**
Castles **86–87,** 87
Caterpillars 57, **57,** 80, **80**
Cats
  crepuscular activity 68
  vertical pupils 6
Chameleons 77, 97, **97**
Charles, Prince of Wales 131
Cheese
  blue cheese 17, **17**
  electricity powered by 170
  grilled cheese sandwiches 153, **153**
  Stilton cheese 65, **65**
  and weird dreams 83
Cheese-Rolling event 124
Cherries 37, **37**
Chewing gum **58,** 59, **59,** 61, 178
Chicken soup 27, **27**
Chili peppers 121, **121**
Chimpanzees 162, 176
China
  birthday traditions 116
  porcelain-dishware statue 178
  rainbow-colored foothills 144, **144, 145**
  wall of trees 73, **73**
  world's largest public bathroom 157
Chinchillas 99, **99**
Chinese legends 56
Chinese New Year 55
Chinese zodiac 63, **63**
Chitin 17
Chocolate
  dresses 8, **8,** 106, **106**
  Easter bunnies 61, **61**
  pudding 121
Chocolate Hills, Philippines 51
Christmas trees 21, **21,** 170, **170**
Churches
  inside tree trunk 21, **21**
  world's smallest 178
Cicadas 39, **39**
Cinderella bed 152, **152**
Cinema, pedal-powered 171, **171**
Cinnabar 50, **50**
Climate: vs. weather 129
Club soda 164
Cockroaches 112
Coffee 119, **119**
Coffins 123, 125
Colors, extra 7
Comets 15, **15**
Computer chips 45, **45**
Constellations 62–63, **62–63,** 126
Contact lenses 47
Cookiecutter sharks 147
Copeland, Misty 163
Corgis 124, **124**
Cornelius, Robert 89, **89**
Crayfish 68, **68**
Crepuscular animals 68
Crested auklets 111
Crickets 56, 108, **108,** 129
Crocodiles 13, 76, **76,** 101, **101**
Crowns 32, **32**
Curious George (character) 177
Cuttlefish 66

D

Dandelions **36,** 37, **79,** 118
Dementor wasps 112, **112**
Deserts 72–73, **72–73**
Diamond Beach, Iceland 33
Diamonds 34, 50, **50,** 153
Didgeridoos 104
Dinosaurs
  Arctic regions 84
  robot receptionist 174, **174**
  T. rex costume 107, **107**
Disney, Walt 87, 101
Disney World, Florida, U.S.A. 93, **93**
Disneyland, California, U.S.A. 101
Diving bell spiders 109, **109**
Dog bathtubs 153, **153**
Dog collars 153
Dog-poop radio transmitters 135
Dogs
  beach day 124, **124**
  burrs in fur 37
  as copycats 67
  intelligence 98
  puppy coats 97
Doldrums 11
Doll, haunted 123, **123**
Dolphins 98, **98**
Donuts, gold-encrusted 153, **153**
Dragon robot 175, **175**
Dragon statue 178
Dragonfly-shaped vehicle 135, **135**
Dragons: Norse legends 30
Dragon's blood trees 21
Dreams and dreaming 31, 82–83
Dresses
  chocolate 8, **8,** 106, **106**
  gummy bear 61, **61**

world's longest wedding dress 9, **9**
Drones 174, **174**
Drums 104, **104**
Dumbo octopuses 172–173, **173**
Dung beetles 37
Durian fruit 121, **121**

E

Earle, Sylvia 162, **162**
Earthquakes 11, 164
Easter bunnies 61, **61**
Easter Island, South Pacific Ocean **126–127,** 127
Eels 14, **14,** 170
Eggplant 121, **121**
Eggs, bird 30, **30, 91**
Egyptians, ancient 63
Einstein, Albert 39, **39,** 82, 143, **143**
El Capitan, Yosemite National Park, California, U.S.A. **132–133,** 133
Electricity 170–171
Elephant, mechanical 100, **100**
Elephants 93, **93,** 105, **105,** 130, **130**
Emeralds 51, **51**
Empire State Building, New York, U.S.A. 19
Endoliths 51
England
  animatronic ape 106, **106**
  haunted places 122
  shark on roof 178, **178–179**
  see also London; Woolpit
Envy: vs. jealousy 129
Eyes 6–7, **6–7,** 25, **25**

F

Fashion 8–9, **8–9**; *see also* Dresses
Feathers 96, 97, 99
Feet
  candles lit by 117
  fish pedicures 25, **25**
  grass-covered flip-flops 159
Fennec foxes 68, **68,** 72, **72**
Ferris wheels 93
Festivals 59, 106, **106,** 120, **120,** 124–125, 159, **159**
Fiberglass 46, **46**
Figure skating 155, **155**
Finland 61, 84
Fire 52–53, **52–53,** 109
Fireflies 16, 68, **146,** 147, **147**
Firefly squid 146
Firenados 52, **52**
Fish 24–25, **24–25**
  anglerfish 146
  baby fish 148, **148**
  eels 14, **14,** 170
  hagfish 91
  parrotfish 44, **44,** 91, **91**
  scales 24, 98
  see also Sharks
Fishing 24, 55
Flamingos 96, **96**
Flip-flops 159, **159**
Fool's gold 35, **35**
Football 25, 132
Four-eyed fish 25, **25**
France
  cheese-powered electricity 170
  church in tree trunk 21, **21**
  gold in lemonade 33, **33**
  theme park 100, **100**
  waterslide 10
  see also Paris
Freckles 14, **14**
Frogs 68, 102, **102**
Fruits 35, **35,** 37, **37,** 115, 120–121, **120–121**
Fulgurite 19
Fuligo septica 91, **91**
Fungi 16–17, **16–17,** 23
Fur 34, 68, 97, 99

G

Garlic 120, **120,** 124
Garnets 50, **50**
Gates, Bill 161
Geckos 94, 96, **96,** 175, **175**
Gelotology 139
Gemstones 32, **32,** 50–51, **50–51**
Gerenuk antelopes 112, **112**
Germans: candy eating 60
Germany
  castle **86–87,** 87
  water park 100
Ghosts 122
Giant squid 6
Gingko tree seeds 120, **120**
Giraffes 180, **181**
Glass 46–47, **46–47**
Glass-bottom boats 142
Glowworms 147, **147**
Goats 6, 13, 68
Goatskin boots 168, **168**
Gobi Desert, Asia 73
Gold
  edible 33, **33,** 65, **65,** 153, **153,** 154
  gold bathtub 34, **34**
  King Tut's mask 33, **33**
  from meteors 35
  Olympic medals 163
Golden lancehead vipers 102
Golden moles 34

Golden orb weaving spiders 56, **56**
Golden tortoise beetles 35
Goldfish 24, **24,** 25
Goodall, Jane 162
Gorilla sculptures 106, **106**
Gorillas 55
Grasshopper sculptures 179
Grasshoppers 129, **129**
Great bustards 103
"Great Green Wall" (trees) 73, **73**
Greek mythology 137
Greeks, ancient 62, 64
Green dye 8
Green sea turtles 55, **55**
Grilled cheese sandwiches 153, **153**
Guitars 104, 105, **175**
Gummy candies 58, 59, **61**
Gummy vitamins 14, 68

H

Haast's eagles 30
Hagfish 91
Hair
  jewelry made from 8, **8**
  vs. fur 164
Hair accessories: live lizards 9
Halloween 60
Harry Potter series 112
Haunted places 122–123, **122–123**
Hawks 66, **66**
Headington, England 178, **178–179**
Heart, human 171
Hedgehogs 141, **141,** 149, **149**
Helicoprion 12
Hermit crabs 66
Himalaya, Asia 144, 166
Hippos 98, **98,** 127, 140, **140,** 148
Honnold, Alex 133, **133**
Hope Diamond 34
Hornets 11, 171, **171**
Horses 42, **42,** 58, 88, **88,** 140, **140**
Hot Water Beach, New Zealand 45
Howler monkeys 176, **176–177**
Hyenas 111, **111**
Hyperion (redwood) 22

I

Ice
  in comets 15
  magician's stunt 130
  truck made of 55, **55**
Ice cream 124
Ice skating **155**
Iceland 33, 84
Insanity (ride) **100–101,** 101
Int-Ball (drone) 174, **174**
International Space Station 47, 157
Ironing, extreme 132, **132**
Italy
  birthday traditions 115
  festival 125
  haunted island 122
  pizza law 64

J

Japan
  aquariums 156, 170
  art installation 159, **159**
  firefly squid 146
  fruit-shaped bus stops 179, **179**
  gold bathtub 34, **34**
  robot-staffed hotel 174, **174**
  snow monkeys 176
  snowball fighting 154, **154**
  traditions 37
  wasabi-flavored candy 59, **59**
Japanese dwarf flying squirrels 140
Jealousy: vs. envy 129
Jell-O 60
Jelly beans 60, **60**
Jellyfish 136–137, **136–137,** 147
Jennings, Kerri Walsh 163
Jervis Bay, Australia **146–147**
Joan of Arc 43, **43**
Jordan, Michael 161, **161**
Joyner-Kersee, Jackie 163

K

Kangaroos 128
Kayaks and kayaking 106, **106,** 132, 155
Kermit the Frog balloon **55**
Kermode bears 151, **151**
Kiribati, South Pacific Ocean 43
KitKat bars 59, **59**
Knights 42, **42,** 43, **43**
Komodo dragons 77, **77, 102–103,** 103

L

Las Vegas, Nevada, U.S.A.
  pizza convention 65
  thrill ride **100–101,** 101
Lasers 47, 50, **50,** 70
Laughter 138–139
Lava 74–75, **74–75**
Lemurs 94, 95
Lettuce 121, **121**
License plates, bear-shaped 151, **151**
Light, balls of 127

Lightning 18–19, **18–19,** 47, 109, **109,** 171, **171**
Limbo skating 132
Limpets 12
Lincoln, Abraham 155, 161
Lindbergh, Charles 161
Lipsticks 98, **98,** 134
Lisicki, Sabine 162
Lithops plants 67
Lizards 9, **9,** 77, **77,** 96, **96**; *see also* Geckos
Llamas 12, **12,** 164
Lobster sculpture 178, **178**
Lobsters: vs. crayfish 68
Loch Ness Monster 127
Lollipops 58, **58**
London, England
  aquarium-dining divers 55, **55**
  art installation 158, **158**
  expensive hamburger 153
  see also Tower Bridge
Lovelace, Ada 163, **163**

M

Madagascar: stone towers 94, **94, 95**
Maddison, Robbie 160, **160**
Madikwe Hills Lodge, South Africa **156–157,** 157
Maggot slime 90
Magicians 130–131, **130–131**
Magma 75
Magpies 34, **34**
Manchineel trees 22
Mangoes 164
Margay cats 67, **67**
Mars (planet) 33, 40, 48
Marshmallows 14, 59, **59**
Maskelyne, Jasper 131
May-Treanor, Misty 163
Maya 35, 97
Meringue 14, **14**
Meteorites 15
Meteors 15, 35
Mexico
  crystal cave 35
  glass-floored restroom 156, **156**
  piñatas 115, **115**
  underwater museum 142, **142**
Mexico City, Mexico: parade 55, **55**
Mica 35
Microwaves 171
Milk, Harvey 161
Mimas (Saturn's moon) 48, **48**
Minerals: vs. vitamins 68
Mirror spiders 35, **35**
Moles: vs. freckles 14
Monkeys 67, 112, **112,** 176–177, **176–177**
Murmurations 31
Museums 142–143, **142–143**
Mushrooms 16, **16,** 17, **17,** 80, **80,** 171, **171**
Musical instruments 104–105, **104–105**
  band of robots 175, **175**
  underwater band 55, **55**
Mustard Museum, Wisconsin, U.S.A. 143, **143**

N

Nanobots 137
Narwhals 113, **113**
National parks 166–167, **166–167**
National Zoo, Washington, D.C. 105, 115, **115**
Neuschwanstein Castle, Germany **86–87,** 87
New Horizons (spacecraft) 49
New York City, New York
  magician's stunt 130
  underground rivers 93
New Zealand
  extinct raptor 30
  "fairy bread" 116, **116**
  glowworm caves 147, **147**
  hot water beach 45
  sheep 99, **99**
Nocturnal animals 68
Norse legends 30
North Star 62
Northwest Territories, Canada: license plate 151, **151**
Norway
  Arctic territory 84
  balls of light 127
  seed vault 37, **37**
Numbers 38–39

O

Obsidian 47
Octopuses 103, **103,** 172–173, **173**
Old Faithful (geyser), Yellowstone National Park, Wyoming, U.S.A. 166
Old Norse (language) 168
Olympics
  figure skating 155, **155**
  torch 53, **53**
  track and field 163
  volleyball 163
Omega (symbol) 39, **39**
Opossums 66, **66,** 68
Oranges 109, 125
Orangutans 22, **22**
Orchid mantises 67, **67**
Osage orange trees: fruit 20, **20**

Ostriches
eggs **91**
toes 31, **31**
Ouija board tombstone 179, **179**
Owls 30, **30,** 66, **66,** 97, **97**

P

Pac-Man 65
Pandas 115, **115**
Pangolins 99, **99**
Papayas 164, **164**
Paris, France
catacombs 93, **93**
chocolate dress 8, **8**
Parrotfish 44, **44,** 91, **91**
Pato 154
Peanut butter 78–79, **78–79,** 136, **136**
Pele's hair 75
Peterson, Patrick 89
Photography 88–89, **88–89**
Pi (number) 39
Pig-shaped race car 106, **106**
Pigeons 135, **135**
Pigs 16, **16**
Piñatas 115, **115**
Pink iguanas 76, **76**
Pink planet 48
Pistachios 53, **53**
Pizza 59, 64–65, **64–65**
Pizza-slice sleeping bag 106, **106**
Plantains 129
Platypuses 170, **170**
Plumicorns 30
Poison 8, **8,** 102, 103
Poison dart frogs 102, **102**
Polar bears **85,** 150, **150,** 151
Portland Vase 47, **47**
Potato-shaped tricycles 159, **159**
Poveglia Island, Italy 122
Presley, Elvis 153, **153**
Pumice stones 74, **74**
Purple (color) 8
Pygmy hippos 140
Pygmy marmosets 140, **140**
Pyrite 35, **35**

Q

Quasars 49, **49**
Quetzals 97, **97**
Quicksand 92

R

Race cars 106, **106,** 118–119, **118–119**
Racquetball 129
Radishes 125, **125**
Rainforests 17, 100, 102
Rainbows 70–71, **70–71**
Rattlesnakes 66, 67
Reagan, Ronald 60
Reptiles 76–77, **76–77**; *see also* Lizards; Snakes
Restrooms 156–157, **156–157**
Ride, Sally 163, **163**
Roadside attractions 178–179, **178–179**
Robots 106, **106,** 137, 152, **152,** 174–175, **174–175**
Rock climbing 94, **132–133,** 133
Rock formations 51, **51,** 144–145, **144–145**
Rocking chairs 155
Roller skating 132
Roman emperors 8, 47
Roosevelt, Eleanor 163, **163**
Roosevelt, Theodore 150, **150**
Roswell, New Mexico, U.S.A. 126
Rubik's Cubes 175, **175**
Russia
Arctic territory 84
birthday pies 117
tumbleweeds 72
water-powered computer 175

S

Sagittarius (constellation) 126
Sahara desert, Africa 73
Salsagheti (candy) 59
Salt 33, 40, 68
Salt and Pepper Shaker Museum, Tennessee, U.S.A. 143
Sand 33, 42, 44, **44–45,** 45, 47
Sand dunes 73
Sandbox trees 37
Sandwiches
grilled cheese 153, **153**
peanut butter and jelly 78–79, **78–79**
Saturn (planet) 48, 70, **70**
Scales
fish 24, 98
pangolins 99, **99**
Scallops 6, **6**
Sea lions 68, **69**
Sea otters 68
Sea slugs **28–29,** 29, 110
Sea snails 12
Sea snakes 14
Sea turtles 55, **55,** 156
Seals 68
Seashores 44–45, **44–45**
Seed-spitting contests 120, **120**
Seed vaults 37, **37**
Seeds 36–37, **36–37**

gingko trees 120, **120**
"moon trees" 21
papayas 164, **165**
Selfies 89, **89**
Serengeti National Park, Tanzania 166
Shackleton, Ernest 108
Shakespeare, William 160
Shark sculpture 178, **178–179**
Sharks 12, **24–25,** 25, **101,** 147, 171, **171**
Sheep 6, **6,** 13, 99, **99,** 109, **109**
Shimmering (waves) 11
Shipwrecks 166, **166**
Shivering 84, 108
Silk 56–57
Silkworms 56, 57, **57**
Silverware, giant 159, **159**
Singapore
durian fruit 121
Supertrees 22, **22**
Sitting Bull (Lakota chief) 160, **160**
Skeleton Coast National Park, Namibia 166, **166**
Skin, human
blue at birth 97
color and carrots 121
freckles vs. moles 14
grown in lab 99
nerve endings 97
shedding 96
sunburn 98
Skunk cabbage 110
Skunks 110, **110**
Skyaking 155
Skydiving 132
Sleep 82–83
Sleeping bags 106, **106**
Slime 14, 90–91
Sloth bears 150, **150,** 151
Sloths 68, 148, **148**
Slugs
vs. snails 14
see also Sea slugs
Smells 40, 48, 110–111
Snails 12, 14, **90,** 102, 140
Snake Island, Brazil 102
Snakes
gliding 76
leg bones 77
pupils 6
venom 14, 102
Snow kayaking 106, **106**
Snow monkeys 176
Snowball fighting 154, **154**
Snub-nosed monkeys 112, **112**
Soccer 107, **107,** 145
SOFAR channel 11
Soil 92, **92–93**
South Africa
outdoor bathtub **156–157,** 157
poop-scented seeds 37
surfing marathon 133
winter waves 155
Southern right whales 112
Space 15, **15,** 21, 48–49, **48–49,** 105, 121; *see also* Astronauts
Spacecraft 47, 48, 49, 58, 157
Sparkling mineral water 164
Spectacled bears 151
Spiders 35, **35,** 56, **56,** 109, **109,** 113
Spies 57, 134–135, **134–135**
Sports 154–155, **154–155**
Spotted Lake, Okanagan Valley, Canada 40, **40, 41**
Sprinkles 116, **116**
Squash (sport) 129
Squid 6, 65, 146, **146**
Stained glass 46, **46–47**
Stanley Hotel, Colorado, U.S.A. 122, **122**
Starlings 31
Stars **15,** 32, 48, 49, 62
Static electricity 170
Stone towers: Madagascar **94,** 94–95, **95**
Strawberries 37
Strawberry-shaped bus stop 179, **179**
Sullenberger, Chesley 161
Sun 14, **18,** 50, 164
Sun bears 151
Sunda flying lemurs 113, **113**
Sundae sculpture 179
Sunlight 27, 171
Surfing 10, **10–11,** 133
Survival 108–109
Swash zone 44

T

Taft, William Howard 122
Tanukis 113, **113**
Taos, New Mexico, U.S.A. 126
Tardigrades 109
Technology 174–175, **174–175**
Teeth 12–13, **12–13**
crocodiles 76, **76**
narwhals 113, **113**
Theta waves 11
Thunder 18
Tidal waves 164
Titan (Saturn's moon) 70
Toads vs. frogs 68
Toast: with sprinkles 116, **116**
Toilets 143, **156,** 157, **157**
Toledo, Ohio, U.S.A. 47
Tomatillos 14, **14**

Tomato sauce 64, 65
Tomatoes 14, 125, **125**
Toothbrushes 13
Tootsie Rolls 61
Tourmaline 51, **51**
Tower Bridge, London, England
  gorilla-costumed runners 55, **55**
  motorcycle stuntman 160, **160**
Toyama Bay, Japan 146
TRAPPIST-1 (dwarf star) 48
Trees 20–23, **20–23,** 73, **73**
Truck made of ice 55, **55**
Truffles 16, **16**
Tsingy de Bemaraha national park and reserve, Madagascar 94, **94, 95**
Tsunamis 11, 148, 164
Tubas 104, **104**
Tumbleweeds 72, **72**
Turkey
  rock formations 51
  whistled language 30
Turtles 55, **55,** 77, **77,** 156
Tutankhamun, King (Egypt)
  death 127
  mask 33, **33**
Typewriters 105, **105**

U

UFOs 126, **126,** 179
Umbrella art 54, **54**
Umpires 155
United Kingdom
  children's book character 177
  crown 32, **32**
  sweetmeats 60, **60**
  see also England
United States
  Arctic territory 84
  Christmas trees 21, **21**
  cicadas 39, **39**
  jewelry made from hair 8
  marshmallows 14
  "moon trees" 21
  peanut butter and jelly 78
  school lunches 65
Urine 42

V

Vegetable Orchestra 105, **105**
Vegetables 65, 105, **105,** 120–121, **120–121**
Velcro 37, 78
Velvet worms 90, **90**
Venezuela
  lightning-prone lake 18
  waterfall **166–167,** 167
Venom 14, 102, 103, 112
Vermilion Cliffs National Monument, Arizona, U.S.A. **2–3,** 50, **50**
Victoria, Queen (United Kingdom) 88
Vikings 56, 168–169, **168–169**
Viruses 26–27, **26–27**
Vitamins 14, 68
Volcanoes 39, **39,** 47, 74, 75, 154, **154–155,** 164
Von der Decken's sifakas 94, **94**
Voynich, Wilfrid 126

W

Wallabies 128, **128**
Washington, George 117, **117**
Water parks 100, 101, **101**
Waterfalls **166–167,** 167
Watermelons 120, **120**
Waves 10–11, **10–11,** 44, 45, 155, 164, **164**
Weather: vs. climate 129
Whale sharks **24–25,** 25
Winfrey, Oprah 162, **162**
Wing-walking 133
Wood tiger moths 102, **102**
Woolpit, England: green children 126
World War I 135
World War II 57, 61, 78, 131, 151

Y

Yellow-bellied sapsuckers 20, **20**
Yellow wagtails **30–31**
Yeti crabs 112
York, England: ghost 122
Yorkshire pudding 124

Z

Z-machines (robot band) 175, **175**
Zero (number) 39
Zhangye Danxia National Geopark, China 144, **144, 145**
Zipper art 159, **159**
Zodiac, Chinese 63, **63**
Zombie worms 103
Zorbs 132

Copyright © 2019 National Geographic Partners, LLC

Published by National Geographic Partners, LLC. All rights reserved.
Reproduction of the whole or any part of the contents without written permission from the publisher is prohibited.

Since 1888, the National Geographic Society has funded more than 12,000 research, exploration, and preservation projects around the world. The Society receives funds from National Geographic Partners, LLC, funded in part by your purchase. A portion of the proceeds from this book supports this vital work. To learn more, visit natgeo.com/info.

NATIONAL GEOGRAPHIC and Yellow Border Design are trademarks of the National Geographic Society, used under license.

For more information, visit nationalgeographic.com, call 1-800-647-5463, or write to the following address:

National Geographic Partners
1145 17th Street N.W.
Washington, D.C. 20036-4688 U.S.A.

Visit us online at nationalgeographic.com/books

For librarians and teachers: ngchildrensbooks.org

More for kids from National Geographic: natgeokids.com

National Geographic Kids magazine inspires children to explore their world with fun yet educational articles on animals, science, nature, and more. Using fresh storytelling and amazing photography, *Nat Geo Kids* shows kids ages 6 to 14 the fascinating truth about the world—and why they should care.
kids.nationalgeographic.com/subscribe

For information about special discounts for bulk purchases, please contact National Geographic Books Special Sales: specialsales@natgeo.com

For rights or permissions inquiries, please contact National Geographic Books Subsidiary Rights: bookrights@natgeo.com

Designed by Chad Tomlinson

The publisher would like to thank everyone who made this book possible: Michaela Weglinski, project editor; Kate Hale, executive editor; Kelly Hargrave and Brittany Moya del Pino, writers; Callie Broaddus, senior designer; Lori Epstein, director of photography; Alison O'Brien Muff, photo editor; Sally Abbey, managing editor; Joan Gossett, editorial production manager; Sophie Massie, fact-checker; and Anne LeongSon and Gus Tello, design production assistants.

Hardcover ISBN: 978-1-4263-3435-1
Reinforced library binding ISBN: 978-1-4263-3436-8

Printed in China
19/PPS/1